Cain: A Mystery by

George Gordon Byron, 6th Baron Byron, but ... just Byron was a leading English poet in the Romantic Movement along with Keats and Shelley.

Byron was born on January 22nd, 1788. He was a great traveller across Europe, spending many years in Italy and much time in Greece. With his aristocratic indulgences, flamboyant style along with his debts, and a string of lovers he was the constant talk of society.

In 1823 he joined the Greeks in their war of Independence against the Ottoman Empire, both helping to fund and advise on the war's conduct.

It was an extraordinary adventure, even by his own standards. But, for us, it is his poetry for which he is mainly remembered even though it is difficult to see where he had time to write his works of immense beauty. But write them he did.

He died on April 19th 1824 after having contracted a cold which, on the advice of his doctors, was treated with blood-letting. This cause complications and a violent fever set in. Byron died like his fellow romantics, tragically young and on some foreign field.

"Now the Serpent was more subtil than any beast of the field which the Lord God had made."
Genesis, Chapter 3rd, verse 1.

Index of Contents

INTRODUCTION TO CAIN

Cain was begun at Ravenna, July 16, and finished September 9, 1821 (vide MS. M.). Six months before, when he was at work on the first act of Sardanapalus, Byron had "pondered" Cain, but it was not till Sardanapalus and a second historical play, The Two Foscari, had been written, copied out, and sent to England, that he indulged his genius with a third drama—on "a metaphysical subject, something in the style of Manfred" (Letters, 1901, v. 189).

Goethe's comment on reading and reviewing Cain was that he should be surprised if Byron did not pursue the treatment of such "biblical subjects," as the destruction of Sodom and Gomorrah (Conversations, etc., 1879, p. 62); and, many years after, he told Crabb Robinson (Diary, 1869, ii. 435) that Byron should have lived "to execute his vocation ... to dramatize the Old Testament." He was better equipped for such a task than might have been imagined. A Scottish schoolboy, "from a child he had known the Scriptures," and, as his Hebrew Melodies testify, he was not unwilling to turn to the Bible as a source of poetic inspiration. Moreover, he was born with the religious temperament. Questions "of Providence, foreknowledge, will and fate," exercised his curiosity because they appealed to his imagination and moved his spirit. He was eager to plunge into controversy with friends and advisers who challenged or rebuked him, Hodgson, for instance, or Dallas; and he responded with remarkable amenity to the strictures and exhortations of such orthodox professors as Mr. Sheppard and Dr. Kennedy. He was, no doubt, from first to last a heretic, impatient, not to say contemptuous, of authority, but he was by no means indifferent to religion altogether. To "argue about it and about" was a necessity, if not an agreeable relief, to his intellectual energies. It would appear from the Ravenna diary (January 28, 1821, Letters, 1901, v. 190,191), that the conception of Lucifer was working in his brain before the "tragedy of Cain" was actually begun. He had been recording a "thought" which had come to him, that "at the very height of human desire and pleasure, a certain sense of doubt and sorrow"—an amari aliquid which links the future to the past, and so blots out the present—"mingles with our bliss," making it of none effect, and, by way of moral or corollary to his soliloquy, he adds three lines of verse headed, "Thought for a speech of Lucifer in the Tragedy of Cain"—

"Were Death an Evil, would I let thee live?
Fool! live as I live—as thy father lives,
And thy son's sons shall live for evermore."

In these three lines, which were not inserted in the play, and in the preceding "thought," we have the key-note to Cain. "Man walketh in a vain shadow"—a shadow which he can never overtake, the shadow of an eternally postponed fruition. With a being capable of infinite satisfaction, he is doomed to realize failure in attainment. In all that is best and most enjoyable, "the rapturous moment and the placid hour," there is a foretaste of "Death the Unknown"! The tragedy of Manfred lies in remorse for the inevitable past; the tragedy of Cain, in revolt against the limitations of the inexorable present. The investigation of the "sources" of Cain does not lead to any very definite conclusion (see Lord Byron's Cain und Seine Quellen, von Alfred Schaffner, 1880). He was pleased to call his play "a Mystery," and, in his Preface (vide post, p. 207), Byron alludes to the Old Mysteries as "those very profane productions, whether in English, French, Italian, or Spanish." The first reprint of the Chester Plays was published by the Roxburghe Club in 1818, but Byron's knowledge of Mystery Plays was probably derived from Dodsley's Plays (ed. 1780, I., xxxiii.-xlii.), or from John Stevens's Continuation of Dugdale's Monasticon (vide post, p. 207), or possibly, as Herr Schaffner suggests, from Warton's History of English Poetry, ed. 1871, ii. 222-230. He may, too, have witnessed some belated Rappresentazione of the Creation and Fall at Ravenna, or in one of the remoter towns or villages of Italy. There is a superficial resemblance between the treatment of the actual encounter of Cain and Abel, and the conventional rendering of the same incident in the Ludus Coventriæ, and in the Mistère du Viel Testament; but it is unlikely that he had closely studied any one Mystery Play at first hand. On the other hand, his recollections of Gessner's Death of Abel which "he had never read since he was eight years old," were clearer than he imagined. Not only in such minor matters as the destruction of Cain's altar by a whirlwind, and the substitution of the Angel of the Lord for the Deus of the Mysteries, but in the Teutonic domesticities of Cain and Adah, and the evangelical piety of Adam and Abel, there is a reflection, if not an imitation, of the German idyll (see Gessner's Death of Abel, ed. 1797, pp. 80, 102).

Of his indebtedness to Milton he makes no formal acknowledgment, but he was not ashamed to shelter himself behind Milton's shield when he was attacked on the score of blasphemy and profanity. "If Cain be blasphemous, Paradise Lost is blasphemous" (letter to Murray, Pisa, February 8, 1822), was, he would fain believe, a conclusive answer to his accusers. But apart from verbal parallels or coincidences, there is a genuine affinity between Byron's Lucifer and Milton's Satan. Lucifer, like Satan, is "not less than Archangel ruined," a repulsed but "unvanquished Titan," marred by a demonic sorrow, a confessor though a rival of Omnipotence. He is a majestic and, as a rule, a serious and solemn spirit, who compels the admiration and possibly the sympathy of the reader. There is, however, another strain in his ghostly attributes, which betrays a more recent consanguinity: now and again he gives token that he is of the lineage of Mephistopheles. He is sometimes, though rarely, a mocking as well as a rebellious spirit, and occasionally indulges in a grim persiflage beneath the dignity if not the capacity of Satan. It is needless to add that Lucifer has a most lifelike personality of his own. The conception of the spirit of evil justifying an eternal antagonism to the Creator from the standpoint of a superior morality, may, perhaps, be traced to a Manichean source, but it has been touched with a new emotion. Milton's devil is an abstraction of infernal pride—

"Sole Positive of Night!
Antipathist of Light!
Fate's only essence! primal scorpion rod—
The one permitted opposite of God!"

Goethe's devil is an abstraction of scorn. He "maketh a mock" alike of good and evil! But Byron's devil is a spirit, yet a mortal too—the traducer, because he has suffered for his sins; the deceiver, because he is self-deceived; the hoper against hope that there is a ransom for the soul in perfect self-will and not in perfect self-sacrifice. Byron did not uphold Lucifer, but he "had passed that way," and could imagine a spiritual warfare not only against the Deus of the Mysteries or of the Book of Genesis, but against what he believed and acknowledged to be the Author and Principle of good.

Autres temps, autres mœurs! It is all but impossible for the modern reader to appreciate the audacity of Cain, or to realize the alarm and indignation which it aroused by its appearance. Byron knew that he was raising a tempest, and pleads, in his Preface, "that with regard to the language of Lucifer, it was difficult for me to make him talk like a clergyman," and again and again he assures his correspondents (e.g. to Murray, November 23, 1821, "Cain is nothing more than a drama;" to Moore, March 4, 1822, "With respect to Religion, can I never convince you that I have no such opinions as the characters in that drama, which seems to have frightened everybody?" Letters, 1901, v. 469; vi. 30) that it is Lucifer and not Byron who puts such awkward questions with regard to the "politics of paradise" and the origin of evil. Nobody seems to have believed him. It was taken for granted that Lucifer was the mouthpiece of Byron, that the author of Don Juan was not "on the side of the angels."

Little need be said of the "literature," the pamphlets and poems which were evoked by the publication of Cain: A Mystery. One of the most prominent assailants (said to be the Rev. H. J. Todd (1763-1845), Archdeacon of Cleveland, 1832, author inter alia of Original Sin, Free Will, etc., 1818) issued A Remonstrance to Mr. John Murray, respecting a Recent Publication, 1822, signed "Oxoniensis." The sting of the Remonstrance lay in the exposure of the fact that Byron was indebted to Bayle's Dictionary for his rabbinical legends, and that he had derived from the same source his

Manichean doctrines of the Two Principles, etc., and other "often-refuted sophisms" with regard to the origin of evil. Byron does not borrow more than a poet and a gentleman is at liberty to acquire by way of raw material, but it cannot be denied that he had read and inwardly digested more than one of Bayle's "most objectionable articles" (e.g. "Adam," "Eve," "Abel," "Manichees," "Paulicians," etc.). The Remonstrance was answered in A Letter to Sir Walter Scott, etc., by "Harroviensis." Byron welcomed such a "Defender of the Faith," and was anxious that Murray should print the letter together with the poem. But Murray belittled the "defender," and was upbraided in turn for his slowness of heart (letter to Murray, June 6, 1822, Letters, 1901, vi. 76).

Fresh combatants rushed into the fray: "Philo-Milton," with a Vindication of the "Paradise Lost" from the charge of exculpating "Cain: A Mystery," London, 1822; "Britannicus," with a pamphlet entitled, Revolutionary Causes, etc., and A Postscript containing Strictures on "Cain," etc., London, 1822, etc.; but their works, which hardly deserve to be catalogued, have perished with them. Finally, in 1830, a barrister named Harding Grant, author of Chancery Practice, compiled a work (Lord Byron's "Cain," etc., with Notes) of more than four hundred pages, in which he treats "the proceedings and speeches of Lucifer with the same earnestness as if they were existing and earthly personages." But it was "a week too late." The "Coryphæus of the Satanic School" had passed away, and the tumult had "dwindled to a calm."

Cain "appeared in conjunction with" Sardanapalus and The Two Foscari, December 19, 1821. Last but not least of the three plays, it had been announced "by a separate advertisement (Morning Chronicle, November 24, 1821), for the purpose of exciting the greater curiosity" (Memoirs of the Life, etc. [by John Watkins], 1822, p. 383), and it was no sooner published than it was pirated. In the following January, "Cain: A Mystery, by the author of Don Juan," was issued by W. Benbow, at Castle Street, Leicester Square (the notorious "Byron Head," which Southey described as "one of those preparatory schools for the brothel and the gallows, where obscenity, sedition, and blasphemy are retailed in drams for the vulgar"!).

Murray had paid Byron £2710 for the three tragedies, and in order to protect the copyright, he applied, through counsel (Lancelot Shadwell, afterwards Vice-Chancellor), for an injunction in Chancery to stop the sale of piratical editions of Cain. In delivering judgment (February 12, 1822), the Chancellor, Lord Eldon (see Courier, Wednesday, February 13), replying to Shadwell, drew a comparison between Cain and Paradise Lost, "which he had read from beginning to end during the course of the last Long Vacation—solicitæ jucunda oblivia vitæ." No one, he argued, could deny that the object and effects of Paradise Lost were "not to bring into disrepute," but "to promote reverence for our religion," and, per contra, no one could affirm that it was impossible to arrive at an opposite conclusion with regard to "the Preface, the poem, the general tone and manner of Cain" It was a question for a jury. A jury might decide that Cain was blasphemous, and void of copyright; and as there was a reasonable doubt in his mind as to the character of the book, and a doubt as to the conclusion at which a jury would arrive, he was compelled to refuse the injunction. According to Dr. Smiles (Memoir of John Murray, 1891, i. 428), the decision of a jury was taken, and an injunction eventually granted. If so, it was ineffectual, for Benbow issued another edition of Cain in 1824 (see Jacob's Reports, p. 474, note). See, too, the case of Murray v. Benbow and Another, as reported in the Examiner, February 17, 1822; and cases of Wolcot v. Walker, Southey v. Sherwood, Murray v. Benbow, and Lawrence v. Smith [Quarterly Review, April, 1822, vol. xxvii. pp. 120-138].

"Cain," said Moore (February 9, 1822), "has made a sensation." Friends and champions, the press, the public "turned up their thumbs." Gifford shook his head; Hobhouse "launched out into a most violent invective" (letter to Murray, November 24, 1821); Jeffrey, in the Edinburgh, was regretful and hortatory; Heber, in the Quarterly, was fault-finding and contemptuous. The "parsons preached at it from Kentish Town to Pisa" (letter to Moore, February 20, 1822). Even "the very highest authority in the land," his Majesty King George IV., "expressed his disapprobation of the blasphemy and licentiousness of Lord Byron's writings" (Examiner, February 17, 1822). Byron himself was forced to admit that "my Mont Saint Jean seems Cain" (Don Juan, Canto XI. stanza lvi. line 2). The many were unanimous in their verdict, but the higher court of the few reversed the judgment.

Goethe said that "Its beauty is such as we shall not see a second time in the world" (Conversations, etc., 1874, p. 261); Scott, in speaking of "the very grand and tremendous drama of Cain," said that the author had "matched Milton on his own ground" (letter to Murray, December 4, 1821, vide post, p. 206); "Cain," wrote Shelley to Gisborne (April 10, 1822), "is apocalyptic; it is a revelation never before communicated to man."

Uncritical praise, as well as uncritical censure, belongs to the past; but the play remains, a singular exercise of "poetic energy," a confession, ex animo, of "the burthen of the mystery,... the heavy and the weary weight Of all this unintelligible world."

For reviews of Cain: A Mystery, vide ante, "Introduction to Sardanapalus," p. 5; see, too, Eclectic Review, May, 1822, N.S. vol. xvii. pp. 418-427; Examiner, June 2, 1822; British Review, 1822, vol. xix. pp. 94-102.

For O'Doherty's parody of the "Pisa" Letter, February 8, 1822, see Blackwood's Edinburgh Magazine, February, 1822, vol. xi. pp. 215-217; and for a review of Harding Grant's Lord Byron's Cain, etc., see Fraser's Magazine, April, 1831, iii. 285-304.

DEDICATION

TO SIR WALTER SCOTT, BART.,
THIS MYSTERY OF CAIN IS INSCRIBED,
BY HIS OBLIGED FRIEND
AND FAITHFUL SERVANT,
THE AUTHOR.

PREFACE

The following scenes are entitled "A Mystery," in conformity with the ancient title annexed to dramas upon similar subjects, which were styled "Mysteries, or Moralities." The author has by no means taken the same liberties with his subject which were common formerly, as may be seen by any reader curious enough to refer to those very profane productions, whether in English, French, Italian, or Spanish. The author has endeavoured to preserve the language adapted to his characters; and where it is (and this is but rarely) taken from actual Scripture, he has made as little alteration, even of words, as the rhythm would permit. The reader will recollect that the book of Genesis does not state that Eve was tempted by a demon, but by "the Serpent;" and that only because he was "the most subtil of all the beasts of the field." Whatever interpretation the Rabbins and the Fathers may have put upon this, I take the words as I find them, and reply, with Bishop Watson upon similar occasions, when the Fathers were quoted to him as Moderator in the schools of Cambridge, "Behold the Book!"—holding up the Scripture. It is to be recollected, that my present subject has nothing to do with the New Testament, to which no reference can be here made without anachronism. With the poems upon similar topics I have not been recently familiar. Since I was twenty I have never read Milton; but I had read him so frequently before, that this may make little difference. Gesner's "Death of Abel" I have never read since I was eight years of age, at Aberdeen. The general impression of my recollection is delight; but of the contents I remember only that Cain's wife was called Mahala, and Abel's Thirza; in the following pages I have called them "Adah" and "Zillah," the earliest female names which occur in Genesis. They were those of Lamech's wives: those of Cain and Abel are not called by their names. Whether, then, a coincidence of subject may have caused the same in expression, I know nothing, and care as little. I am prepared to be accused of Manicheism, or some other hard name ending in ism, which makes a formidable figure and awful sound in the eyes and ears of those who would be as much puzzled to explain the terms so bandied about, as the liberal and pious indulgers in such epithets. Against such I can defend myself, or, if necessary, I can attack in turn. "Claw for claw, as Conan said to Satan and the deevil take the shortest nails" (Waverley).

The reader will please to bear in mind (what few choose to recollect), that there is no allusion to a future state in any of the books of Moses, nor indeed in the Old Testament. For a reason for this extraordinary omission he may consult Warburton's "Divine Legation;" whether satisfactory or not, no better has yet been assigned. I have therefore supposed it new to Cain, without, I hope, any perversion of Holy Writ.

With regard to the language of Lucifer, it was difficult for me to make him talk like a clergyman upon the same subjects; but I have done what I could to restrain him within the bounds of spiritual politeness. If he disclaims having tempted Eve in the shape of the Serpent, it is only because the book of Genesis has not the most distant allusion to anything of the kind, but merely to the Serpent in his serpentine capacity.

Note.—The reader will perceive that the author has partly adopted in this poem the notion of Cuvier, that the world had been destroyed several times before the creation of man. This speculation, derived from the different strata and the bones of enormous and unknown animals found in them, is not contrary to the Mosaic account, but rather confirms it; as no human bones have yet been discovered in those strata, although those of many known animals are found near the remains of the unknown. The assertion of Lucifer, that the pre-Adamite world was also peopled by rational beings much more intelligent than man, and proportionably powerful to the mammoth, etc., etc., is, of course, a poetical fiction to help him to make out his case.

I ought to add, that there is a "tramelogedia" of Alfieri, called "Abele." I have never read that, nor any other of the posthumous works of the writer, except his Life.

RAVENNA, Sept. 20, 1821.

DRAMATIS PERSONÆ

MEN
ADAM
CAIN
ABEL
SPIRITS
ANGEL OF THE LORD
LUCIFER
WOMEN

EVE
ADAH
ZILLAH

ACT I

SCENE I. The Land Without Paradise.

Time, Sunrise.

ADAM, EVE, CAIN, ABEL, ADAH, ZILLAH, offering a Sacrifice.

ADAM - God, the Eternal! Infinite! All-wise!—
Who out of darkness on the deep didst make
Light on the waters with a word—All Hail!
Jehovah! with returning light—All Hail!

EVE - God! who didst name the day, and separate
Morning from night, till then divided never—
Who didst divide the wave from wave, and call
Part of thy work the firmament—All Hail!

ABEL - God! who didst call the elements into
Earth, ocean, air and fire—and with the day
And night, and worlds which these illuminate,
Or shadow, madest beings to enjoy them,
And love both them and thee—All Hail! All Hail!

ADAH - God! the Eternal parent of all things!
Who didst create these best and beauteous beings,
To be belovéd, more than all, save thee—
Let me love thee and them:—All Hail! All Hail!

ZILLAH - Oh, God! who loving, making, blessing all,
Yet didst permit the Serpent to creep in,
And drive my father forth from Paradise,
Keep us from further evil:—Hail! All Hail!

ADAM - Son Cain! my first-born—wherefore art thou silent?

CAIN - Why should I speak?

ADAM - To pray.

CAIN - Have ye not prayed?

ADAM - We have, most fervently.

CAIN - And loudly: I
Have heard you.

ADAM - So will God, I trust.

ABEL - Amen!

ADAM - But thou my eldest born? art silent still?

CAIN - 'Tis better I should be so.

ADAM - Wherefore so?

CAIN - I have nought to ask.

ADAM - Nor aught to thank for?

CAIN - No.

ADAM - Dost thou not live?

CAIN - Must I not die?

EVE - Alas!
The fruit of our forbidden tree begins
To fall.

ADAM - And we must gather it again.
Oh God! why didst thou plant the tree of knowledge?

CAIN - And wherefore plucked ye not the tree of life?
Ye might have then defied him.

ADAM - Oh! my son,
Blaspheme not: these are Serpent's words.

CAIN - Why not?
The snake spoke truth; it was the Tree of Knowledge;
It was the Tree of Life: knowledge is good,
And Life is good; and how can both be evil?

EVE - My boy! thou speakest as I spoke in sin,
Before thy birth: let me not see renewed
My misery in thine. I have repented.
Let me not see my offspring fall into
The snares beyond the walls of Paradise,
Which even in Paradise destroyed his parents.
Content thee with what is. Had we been so,
Thou now hadst been contented.—Oh, my son!

ADAM - Our orisons completed, let us hence,
Each to his task of toil—not heavy, though
Needful: the earth is young, and yields us kindly
Her fruits with little labour.

EVE - Cain—my son—
Behold thy father cheerful and resigned—
And do as he doth.

[Exeunt ADAM and EVE.

ZILLAH - Wilt thou not, my brother?

ABEL -Why wilt thou wear this gloom upon thy brow,
Which can avail thee nothing, save to rouse
The Eternal anger?

ADAH - My belovéd Cain
Wilt thou frown even on me?

CAIN - No, Adah! no;
I fain would be alone a little while.
Abel, I'm sick at heart; but it will pass;
Precede me, brother—I will follow shortly.
And you, too, sisters, tarry not behind;
Your gentleness must not be harshly met:
I'll follow you anon.

ADAH - If not, I will
Return to seek you here.

ABEL - The peace of God
Be on your spirit, brother!

[Exeunt ABEL, ZILLAH, and ADAH.

CAIN - (solus) And this is
Life?—Toil! and wherefore should I toil?—because
My father could not keep his place in Eden?
What had I done in this?—I was unborn:
I sought not to be born; nor love the state
To which that birth has brought me. Why did he
Yield to the Serpent and the woman? or
Yielding—why suffer? What was there in this?
The tree was planted, and why not for him?
If not, why place him near it, where it grew
The fairest in the centre? They have but
One answer to all questions, "'Twas his will,
And he is good." How know I that? Because
He is all-powerful, must all-good, too, follow?

I judge but by the fruits—and they are bitter—
Which I must feed on for a fault not mine.
Whom have we here?—A shape like to the angels
Yet of a sterner and a sadder aspect
Of spiritual essence: why do I quake?
Why should I fear him more than other spirits,
Whom I see daily wave their fiery swords
Before the gates round which I linger oft,
In Twilight's hour, to catch a glimpse of those
Gardens which are my just inheritance,
Ere the night closes o'er the inhibited walls
And the immortal trees which overtop
The Cherubim-defended battlements?
If I shrink not from these, the fire-armed angels,
Why should I quail from him who now approaches?
Yet—he seems mightier far than them, nor less
Beauteous, and yet not all as beautiful
As he hath been, and might be: sorrow seems
Half of his immortality. And is it
So? and can aught grieve save Humanity?
He cometh.

Enter LUCIFER.

LUCIFER - Mortal!

CAIN - Spirit, who art thou?

LUCIFER - Master of spirits.

CAIN - And being so, canst thou
Leave them, and walk with dust?

LUCIFER - I know the thoughts
Of dust, and feel for it, and with you.

CAIN - How!
You know my thoughts?

LUCIFER - They are the thoughts of all
Worthy of thought;—'tis your immortal part
Which speaks within you.

CAIN - What immortal part?
This has not been revealed: the Tree of Life
Was withheld from us by my father's folly,
While that of Knowledge, by my mother's haste,
Was plucked too soon; and all the fruit is Death!

LUCIFER - They have deceived thee; thou shalt live.

CAIN - I live,
But live to die; and, living, see no thing
To make death hateful, save an innate clinging,
A loathsome, and yet all invincible
Instinct of life, which I abhor, as I
Despise myself, yet cannot overcome—
And so I live. Would I had never lived!

LUCIFER -Thou livest—and must live for ever. Think not
The Earth, which is thine outward cov'ring, is
Existence—it will cease—and thou wilt be—
No less than thou art now.

CAIN - No less! and why
No more?

LUCIFER - It may be thou shalt be as we.

CAIN - And ye?

LUCIFER - Are everlasting.

CAIN - Are ye happy?

LUCIFER - We are mighty.

CAIN - Are ye happy?

LUCIFER - No: art thou?

CAIN - How should I be so? Look on me!

LUCIFER - Poor clay!
And thou pretendest to be wretched! Thou!

CAIN - I am:—and thou, with all thy might, what art thou?

LUCIFER - One who aspired to be what made thee, and
Would not have made thee what thou art.

CAIN - Ah!
Thou look'st almost a god; and—

LUCIFER - I am none:
And having failed to be one, would be nought
Save what I am. He conquered; let him reign!

CAIN - Who?

LUCIFER - Thy Sire's maker—and the Earth's.

CAIN - And Heaven's,
And all that in them is. So I have heard
His Seraphs sing; and so my father saith.

LUCIFER - They say—what they must sing and say, on pain
Of being that which I am,—and thou art—
Of spirits and of men.

CAIN - And what is that?

LUCIFER - Souls who dare use their immortality—
Souls who dare look the Omnipotent tyrant in
His everlasting face, and tell him that
His evil is not good! If he has made,
As he saith—which I know not, nor believe—
But, if he made us—he cannot unmake:
We are immortal!—nay, he'd have us so,
That he may torture:—let him! He is great—
But, in his greatness, is no happier than
We in our conflict! Goodness would not make
Evil; and what else hath he made? But let him
Sit on his vast and solitary throne—
Creating worlds, to make eternity
Less burthensome to his immense existence
And unparticipated solitude;
Let him crowd orb on orb: he is alone
Indefinite, Indissoluble Tyrant;
Could he but crush himself, 'twere the best boon
He ever granted: but let him reign on!
And multiply himself in misery!
Spirits and Men, at least we sympathise—
And, suffering in concert, make our pangs
Innumerable, more endurable,
By the unbounded sympathy of all
With all! But He! so wretched in his height,
So restless in his wretchedness, must still
Create, and re-create—perhaps he'll make
One day a Son unto himself—as he
Gave you a father—and if he so doth,
Mark me! that Son will be a sacrifice!

CAIN - Thou speak'st to me of things which long have swum
In visions through my thought: I never could
Reconcile what I saw with what I heard.
My father and my mother talk to me
Of serpents, and of fruits and trees: I see
The gates of what they call their Paradise
Guarded by fiery-sworded Cherubim,
Which shut them out—and me: I feel the weight
Of daily toil, and constant thought: I look
Around a world where I seem nothing, with

Thoughts which arise within me, as if they
Could master all things—but I thought alone
This misery was mine. My father is
Tamed down; my mother has forgot the mind
Which made her thirst for knowledge at the risk
Of an eternal curse; my brother is
A watching shepherd boy, who offers up
The firstlings of the flock to him who bids
The earth yield nothing to us without sweat;
My sister Zillah sings an earlier hymn
Than the birds' matins; and my Adah—my
Own and belovéd—she, too, understands not
The mind which overwhelms me: never till
Now met I aught to sympathise with me.
'Tis well—I rather would consort with spirits.

LUCIFER - And hadst thou not been fit by thine own soul
For such companionship, I would not now
Have stood before thee as I am: a serpent
Had been enough to charm ye, as before.

CAIN - Ah! didst thou tempt my mother?

LUCIFER - I tempt none,
Save with the truth: was not the Tree, the Tree
Of Knowledge? and was not the Tree of Life
Still fruitful? Did I bid her pluck them not?
Did I plant things prohibited within
The reach of beings innocent, and curious
By their own innocence? I would have made ye
Gods; and even He who thrust ye forth, so thrust ye
Because "ye should not eat the fruits of life,
And become gods as we." Were those his words?

CAIN - They were, as I have heard from those who heard them,
In thunder.

LUCIFER - Then who was the Demon? He
Who would not let ye live, or he who would
Have made ye live for ever, in the joy
And power of Knowledge?

CAIN - Would they had snatched both
The fruits, or neither!

LUCIFER - One is yours already,
The other may be still.

CAIN - How so?

LUCIFER - By being

Yourselves, in your resistance. Nothing can
Quench the mind, if the mind will be itself
And centre of surrounding things—'tis made
To sway.

CAIN - But didst thou tempt my parents?

LUCIFER - I?
Poor clay—what should I tempt them for, or how?

CAIN - They say the Serpent was a spirit.

LUCIFER - Who
Saith that? It is not written so on high:
The proud One will not so far falsify,
Though man's vast fears and little vanity
Would make him cast upon the spiritual nature
His own low failing. The snake was the snake—
No more; and yet not less than those he tempted,
In nature being earth also—more in wisdom,
Since he could overcome them, and foreknew
The knowledge fatal to their narrow joys.
Think'st thou I'd take the shape of things that die?

CAIN - But the thing had a demon?

LUCIFER - He but woke one
In those he spake to with his forky tongue.
I tell thee that the Serpent was no more
Than a mere serpent: ask the Cherubim
Who guard the tempting tree. When thousand ages
Have rolled o'er your dead ashes, and your seed's,
The seed of the then world may thus array
Their earliest fault in fable, and attribute
To me a shape I scorn, as I scorn all
That bows to him, who made things but to bend
Before his sullen, sole eternity;
But we, who see the truth, must speak it. Thy
Fond parents listened to a creeping thing,
And fell. For what should spirits tempt them? What
Was there to envy in the narrow bounds
Of Paradise, that spirits who pervade
Space—but I speak to thee of what thou know'st not,
With all thy Tree of Knowledge.

CAIN - But thou canst not
Speak aught of Knowledge which I would not know,
And do not thirst to know, and bear a mind
To know.

LUCIFER - And heart to look on?

CAIN - Be it proved.

LUCIFER - Darest thou look on Death?

CAIN - He has not yet
Been seen.

LUCIFER -But must be undergone.

CAIN - My father
Says he is something dreadful, and my mother
Weeps when he's named; and Abel lifts his eyes
To Heaven, and Zillah casts hers to the earth,
And sighs a prayer; and Adah looks on me,
And speaks not.

LUCIFER - And thou?

CAIN - Thoughts unspeakable
Crowd in my breast to burning, when I hear
Of this almighty Death, who is, it seems,
Inevitable. Could I wrestle with him?
I wrestled with the lion, when a boy,
In play, till he ran roaring from my gripe.

LUCIFER - It has no shape; but will absorb all things
That bear the form of earth-born being.

CAIN - Ah!
I thought it was a being: who could do
Such evil things to beings save a being?

LUCIFER - Ask the Destroyer.

CAIN - Who?

LUCIFER - The Maker—Call him
Which name thou wilt: he makes but to destroy.

CAIN - I knew not that, yet thought it, since I heard
Of Death: although I know not what it is—
Yet it seems horrible. I have looked out
In the vast desolate night in search of him;
And when I saw gigantic shadows in
The umbrage of the walls of Eden, chequered
By the far-flashing of the Cherubs' swords,
I watched for what I thought his coming; for
With fear rose longing in my heart to know
What 'twas which shook us all—but nothing came.
And then I turned my weary eyes from off

Our native and forbidden Paradise,
Up to the lights above us, in the azure,
Which are so beautiful: shall they, too, die?

LUCIFER - Perhaps—but long outlive both thine and thee.

CAIN - I'm glad of that: I would not have them die—
They are so lovely. What is Death? I fear,
I feel, it is a dreadful thing; but what,
I cannot compass: 'tis denounced against us,
Both them who sinned and sinned not, as an ill—
What ill?

LUCIFER - To be resolved into the earth.

CAIN - But shall I know it?

LUCIFER - As I know not death,
I cannot answer.

CAIN - Were I quiet earth,
That were no evil: would I ne'er had been
Aught else but dust!

LUCIFER - That is a grovelling wish,
Less than thy father's—for he wished to know!

CAIN - But not to live—or wherefore plucked he not
The Life-tree?

LUCIFER - He was hindered.

CAIN - Deadly error!
Not to snatch first that fruit:—but ere he plucked
The knowledge, he was ignorant of Death.
Alas! I scarcely now know what it is,
And yet I fear it—fear I know not what!

LUCIFER - And I, who know all things, fear nothing; see
What is true knowledge.

CAIN - Wilt thou teach me all?

LUCIFER - Aye, upon one condition.

CAIN - Name it.

LUCIFER - That
Thou dost fall down and worship me—thy Lord.

CAIN - Thou art not the Lord my father worships.

LUCIFER - No.

CAIN - His equal?

LUCIFER - No;—I have nought in common with him!
Nor would: I would be aught above—beneath—
Aught save a sharer or a servant of
His power. I dwell apart; but I am great:—
Many there are who worship me, and more
Who shall—be thou amongst the first.

CAIN - I never
As yet have bowed unto my father's God.
Although my brother Abel oft implores
That I would join with him in sacrifice:—
Why should I bow to thee?

LUCIFER - Hast thou ne'er bowed
To him?

CAIN - Have I not said it?—need I say it?
Could not thy mighty knowledge teach thee that?

LUCIFER - He who bows not to him has bowed to me.

CAIN - But I will bend to neither.

LUCIFER - Ne'er the less,
Thou art my worshipper; not worshipping
Him makes thee mine the same.

CAIN - And what is that?

LUCIFER - Thou'lt know here—and hereafter.

CAIN - Let me but
Be taught the mystery of my being.

LUCIFER - Follow
Where I will lead thee.

CAIN - But I must retire
To till the earth—for I had promised—

LUCIFER - What?

CAIN - To cull some first-fruits.

LUCIFER - Why?

CAIN - To offer up
With Abel on an altar.

LUCIFER - Said'st thou not
Thou ne'er hadst bent to him who made thee?

CAIN - Yes—
But Abel's earnest prayer has wrought upon me;
The offering is more his than mine—and Adah—

LUCIFER - Why dost thou hesitate?

CAIN - She is my sister,
Born on the same day, of the same womb; and
She wrung from me, with tears, this promise; and
Rather than see her weep, I would, methinks,
Bear all—and worship aught.

LUCIFER - Then follow me!

CAIN - I will.

Enter ADAH.

ADAH - My brother, I have come for thee;
It is our hour of rest and joy—and we
Have less without thee. Thou hast laboured not
This morn; but I have done thy task: the fruits
Are ripe, and glowing as the light which ripens:
Come away.

CAIN - Seest thou not?

ADAH - I see an angel;
We have seen many: will he share our hour
Of rest?—he is welcome.

CAIN - But he is not like
The angels we have seen.

ADAH - Are there, then, others?
But he is welcome, as they were: they deigned
To be our guests—will he?

CAIN - (to LUCIFER) Wilt thou?

LUCIFER - I ask
Thee to be mine.

CAIN - I must away with him.

ADAH - And leave us?

CAIN - Aye.

ADAH - And me?

CAIN - Belovéd Adah!

ADAH - Let me go with thee.

LUCIFER - No, she must not.

ADAH - Who
Art thou that steppest between heart and heart?

CAIN - He is a God.

ADAH - How know'st thou?

CAIN - He speaks like
A God.

ADAH - So did the Serpent, and it lied.

LUCIFER - Thou errest, Adah!—was not the Tree that
Of Knowledge?

ADAH - Aye—to our eternal sorrow.

LUCIFER - And yet that grief is knowledge—so he lied not:
And if he did betray you, 'twas with Truth;
And Truth in its own essence cannot be
But good.

ADAH - But all we know of it has gathered
Evil on ill; expulsion from our home,
And dread, and toil, and sweat, and heaviness;
Remorse of that which was—and hope of that
Which cometh not. Cain! walk not with this Spirit.
Bear with what we have borne, and love me—I
Love thee.

LUCIFER - More than thy mother, and thy sire?

ADAH - I do. Is that a sin, too?

LUCIFER - No, not yet;
It one day will be in your children.

ADAH - What!
Must not my daughter love her brother Enoch?

LUCIFER - Not as thou lovest Cain.

ADAH - Oh, my God!
Shall they not love and bring forth things that love
Out of their love? have they not drawn their milk
Out of this bosom? was not he, their father,
Born of the same sole womb, in the same hour
With me? did we not love each other? and
In multiplying our being multiply
Things which will love each other as we love
Them?—And as I love thee, my Cain! go not
Forth with this spirit; he is not of ours.

LUCIFER - The sin I speak of is not of my making,
And cannot be a sin in you—whate'er
It seem in those who will replace ye in
Mortality.

ADAH - What is the sin which is not
Sin in itself? Can circumstance make sin
Or virtue?—if it doth, we are the slaves
Of—

LUCIFER - Higher things than ye are slaves: and higher
Than them or ye would be so, did they not
Prefer an independency of torture
To the smooth agonies of adulation,
In hymns and harpings, and self-seeking prayers,
To that which is omnipotent, because
It is omnipotent, and not from love,
But terror and self-hope.

ADAH - Omnipotence
Must be all goodness.

LUCIFER - Was it so in Eden?

ADAH - Fiend! tempt me not with beauty; thou art fairer
Than was the Serpent, and as false.

LUCIFER - As true.
Ask Eve, your mother: bears she not the knowledge
Of good and evil?

ADAH - Oh, my mother! thou
Hast plucked a fruit more fatal to thine offspring
Than to thyself; thou at the least hast passed
Thy youth in Paradise, in innocent
And happy intercourse with happy spirits:
But we, thy children, ignorant of Eden,

Are girt about by demons, who assume
The words of God, and tempt us with our own
Dissatisfied and curious thoughts—as thou
Wert worked on by the snake, in thy most flushed
And heedless, harmless wantonness of bliss.
I cannot answer this immortal thing
Which stands before me; I cannot abhor him;
I look upon him with a pleasing fear,
And yet I fly not from him: in his eye
There is a fastening attraction which
Fixes my fluttering eyes on his; my heart
Beats quick; he awes me, and yet draws me near,
Nearer and nearer:—Cain—Cain—save me from him!

CAIN - What dreads my Adah? This is no ill spirit.

ADAH - He is not God—nor God's: I have beheld
The Cherubs and the Seraphs; he looks not
Like them.

CAIN - But there are spirits loftier still—
The archangels.

LUCIFER - And still loftier than the archangels.

ADAH - Aye—but not blesséd.

LUCIFER - If the blessedness
Consists in slavery—no.

ADAH - I have heard it said,
The Seraphs love most—Cherubim know most—
And this should be a Cherub—since he loves not.

LUCIFER - And if the higher knowledge quenches love,
What must he be you cannot love when known?
Since the all-knowing Cherubim love least,
The Seraphs' love can be but ignorance:
That they are not compatible, the doom
Of thy fond parents, for their daring, proves.
Choose betwixt Love and Knowledge—since there is
No other choice: your sire hath chosen already:
His worship is but fear.

ADAH - Oh, Cain! choose Love.

CAIN - For thee, my Adah, I choose not—It was
Born with me—but I love nought else.

ADAH - Our parents?

CAIN - Did they love us when they snatched from the Tree
That which hath driven us all from Paradise?

ADAH - We were not born then—and if we had been,
Should we not love them—and our children, Cain?

CAIN - My little Enoch! and his lisping sister!
Could I but deem them happy, I would half
Forget—but it can never be forgotten
Through thrice a thousand generations! never
Shall men love the remembrance of the man
Who sowed the seed of evil and mankind
In the same hour! They plucked the tree of science
And sin—and, not content with their own sorrow,
Begot me—thee—and all the few that are,
And all the unnumbered and innumerable
Multitudes, millions, myriads, which may be,
To inherit agonies accumulated
By ages!—and I must be sire of such things!
Thy beauty and thy love—my love and joy,
The rapturous moment and the placid hour,
All we love in our children and each other,
But lead them and ourselves through many years
Of sin and pain—or few, but still of sorrow,
Interchecked with an instant of brief pleasure,
To Death—the unknown! Methinks the Tree of Knowledge
Hath not fulfilled its promise:—if they sinned,
At least they ought to have known all things that are
Of knowledge—and the mystery of Death.
What do they know?—that they are miserable.
What need of snakes and fruits to teach us that?

ADAH - I am not wretched, Cain, and if thou
Wert happy—

CAIN - Be thou happy, then, alone—
I will have nought to do with happiness,
Which humbles me and mine.

ADAH - Alone I could not,
Nor would be happy; but with those around us
I think I could be so, despite of Death,
Which, as I know it not, I dread not, though
It seems an awful shadow—if I may
Judge from what I have heard.

LUCIFER - And thou couldst not
Alone, thou say'st, be happy?

ADAH - Alone! Oh, my God!
Who could be happy and alone, or good?

To me my solitude seems sin; unless
When I think how soon I shall see my brother,
His brother, and our children, and our parents.

LUCIFER - Yet thy God is alone; and is he happy?
Lonely, and good?

ADAH - He is not so; he hath
The angels and the mortals to make happy,
And thus becomes so in diffusing joy.
What else can joy be, but the spreading joy?

LUCIFER - Ask of your sire, the exile fresh from Eden;
Or of his first-born son: ask your own heart;
It is not tranquil.

ADAH - Alas! no! and you—
Are you of Heaven?

LUCIFER - If I am not, enquire
The cause of this all-spreading happiness
(Which you proclaim) of the all-great and good
Maker of life and living things; it is
His secret, and he keeps it. We must bear,
And some of us resist—and both in vain,
His Seraphs say: but it is worth the trial,
Since better may not be without: there is
A wisdom in the spirit, which directs
To right, as in the dim blue air the eye
Of you, young mortals, lights at once upon
The star which watches, welcoming the morn.

ADAH - It is a beautiful star; I love it for
Its beauty.

LUCIFER - And why not adore?

ADAH - Our father
Adores the Invisible only.

LUCIFER - But the symbols
Of the Invisible are the loveliest
Of what is visible; and yon bright star
Is leader of the host of Heaven.

ADAH - Our father
Saith that he has beheld the God himself
Who made him and our mother.

LUCIFER - Hast thou seen him?

ADAH - Yes—in his works.

LUCIFER - But in his being?

ADAH - No—
Save in my father, who is God's own image;
Or in his angels, who are like to thee—
And brighter, yet less beautiful and powerful
In seeming: as the silent sunny noon,
All light, they look upon us; but thou seem'st
Like an ethereal night, where long white clouds
Streak the deep purple, and unnumbered stars
Spangle the wonderful mysterious vault
With things that look as if they would be suns;
So beautiful, unnumbered, and endearing,
Not dazzling, and yet drawing us to them,
They fill my eyes with tears, and so dost thou.
Thou seem'st unhappy: do not make us so,
And I will weep for thee.

LUCIFER - Alas! those tears!
Couldst thou but know what oceans will be shed—

ADAH - By me?

LUCIFER - By all.

ADAH - What all?

LUCIFER - The million millions—
The myriad myriads—the all-peopled earth—
The unpeopled earth—and the o'er-peopled Hell,
Of which thy bosom is the germ.

ADAH - O Cain!
This spirit curseth us.

CAIN - Let him say on;
Him will I follow.

ADAH - Whither?

LUCIFER - To a place
Whence he shall come back to thee in an hour;
But in that hour see things of many days.

ADAH - How can that be?

LUCIFER - Did not your Maker make
Out of old worlds this new one in few days?
And cannot I, who aided in this work,

Show in an hour what he hath made in many,
Or hath destroyed in few?

CAIN - Lead on.

ADAH - Will he,
In sooth, return within an hour?

LUCIFER - He shall.
With us acts are exempt from time, and we
Can crowd eternity into an hour,
Or stretch an hour into eternity:
We breathe not by a mortal measurement—
But that's a mystery. Cain, come on with me.

ADAH - Will he return?

LUCIFER - Aye, woman! he alone
Of mortals from that place (the first and last
Who shall return, save ONE), shall come back to thee,
To make that silent and expectant world
As populous as this: at present there
Are few inhabitants.

ADAH - Where dwellest thou?

LUCIFER - Throughout all space. Where should I dwell? Where are
Thy God or Gods—there am I: all things are
Divided with me: Life and Death—and Time—
Eternity—and heaven and earth—and that
Which is not heaven nor earth, but peopled with
Those who once peopled or shall people both—
These are my realms! so that I do divide
His, and possess a kingdom which is not
His. If I were not that which I have said,
Could I stand here? His angels are within
Your vision.

ADAH - So they were when the fair Serpent
Spoke with our mother first.

LUCIFER - Cain! thou hast heard.
If thou dost long for knowledge, I can satiate
That thirst; nor ask thee to partake of fruits
Which shall deprive thee of a single good
The Conqueror has left thee. Follow me.

CAIN - Spirit, I have said it.

[Exeunt LUCIFER and CAIN.

ADAH - (follows exclaiming) Cain! my brother! Cain!

SCENE I. The Abyss of Space.

CAIN - I tread on air, and sink not—yet I fear
To sink.

LUCIFER - Have faith in me, and thou shalt be
Borne on the air, of which I am the Prince.

CAIN - Can I do so without impiety?

LUCIFER - Believe—and sink not! doubt—and perish! thus
Would run the edict of the other God,
Who names me Demon to his angels; they
Echo the sound to miserable things,
Which, knowing nought beyond their shallow senses,
Worship the word which strikes their ear, and deem
Evil or good what is proclaimed to them
In their abasement. I will have none such:
Worship or worship not, thou shalt behold
The worlds beyond thy little world, nor be
Amerced for doubts beyond thy little life,
With torture of my dooming. There will come
An hour, when, tossed upon some water-drops,
A man shall say to a man, "Believe in me,
And walk the waters;" and the man shall walk
The billows and be safe. I will not say,
Believe in me, as a conditional creed
To save thee; but fly with me o'er the gulf
Of space an equal flight, and I will show
What thou dar'st not deny,—the history
Of past—and present, and of future worlds.

CAIN - Oh God! or Demon! or whate'er thou art,
Is yon our earth?

LUCIFER - Dost thou not recognise
The dust which formed your father?

CAIN - Can it be?
Yon small blue circle, swinging in far ether,
With an inferior circlet purpler it still,
Which looks like that which lit our earthly night?
Is this our Paradise? Where are its walls,
And they who guard them?

LUCIFER - Point me out the site
Of Paradise.

CAIN - How should I? As we move
Like sunbeams onward, it grows small and smaller,
And as it waxes little, and then less,
Gathers a halo round it, like the light
Which shone the roundest of the stars, when I
Beheld them from the skirts of Paradise:
Methinks they both, as we recede from them,
Appear to join the innumerable stars
Which are around us; and, as we move on,
Increase their myriads.

LUCIFER - And if there should be
Worlds greater than thine own—inhabited
By greater things—and they themselves far more
In number than the dust of thy dull earth,
Though multiplied to animated atoms,
All living—and all doomed to death—and wretched,
What wouldst thou think?

CAIN - I should be proud of thought
Which knew such things.

LUCIFER - But if that high thought were
Linked to a servile mass of matter—and,
Knowing such things, aspiring to such things,
And science still beyond them, were chained down
To the most gross and petty paltry wants,
All foul and fulsome—and the very best
Of thine enjoyments a sweet degradation,
A most enervating and filthy cheat
To lure thee on to the renewal of
Fresh souls and bodies, all foredoomed to be
As frail, and few so happy—

CAIN - Spirit! I
Know nought of Death, save as a dreadful thing
Of which I have heard my parents speak, as of
A hideous heritage I owe to them
No less than life—a heritage not happy,
If I may judge, till now. But, Spirit! if
It be as thou hast said (and I within
Feel the prophetic torture of its truth),
Here let me die: for to give birth to those
Who can but suffer many years, and die—
Methinks is merely propagating Death,
And multiplying murder.

LUCIFER - Thou canst not
All die—there is what must survive.

CAIN - The Other
Spake not of this unto my father, when
He shut him forth from Paradise, with death
Written upon his forehead. But at least
Let what is mortal of me perish, that
I may be in the rest as angels are.

LUCIFER - I am angelic: wouldst thou be as I am?

CAIN - I know not what thou art: I see thy power,
And see thou show'st me things beyond my power,
Beyond all power of my born faculties,
Although inferior still to my desires
And my conceptions.

LUCIFER - What are they which dwell
So humbly in their pride, as to sojourn
With worms in clay?

CAIN - And what art thou who dwellest
So haughtily in spirit, and canst range
Nature and immortality—and yet
Seem'st sorrowful?

LUCIFER - I seem that which I am;
And therefore do I ask of thee, if thou
Wouldst be immortal?

CAIN - Thou hast said, I must be
Immortal in despite of me. I knew not
This until lately—but since it must be,
Let me, or happy or unhappy, learn
To anticipate my immortality.

LUCIFER -Thou didst before I came upon thee.

CAIN - How?

LUCIFER - By suffering.

CAIN - And must torture be immortal?

LUCIFER - We and thy sons will try. But now, behold!
Is it not glorious?

CAIN - Oh thou beautiful
And unimaginable ether! and
Ye multiplying masses of increased

And still-increasing lights! what are ye? what
Is this blue wilderness of interminable
Air, where ye roll along, as I have seen
The leaves along the limpid streams of Eden?
Is your course measured for ye? Or do ye
Sweep on in your unbounded revelry
Through an aërial universe of endless
Expansion—at which my soul aches to think—
Intoxicated with eternity?
Oh God! Oh Gods! or whatsoe'er ye are!
How beautiful ye are! how beautiful
Your works, or accidents, or whatsoe'er
They may be! Let me die, as atoms die,
(If that they die), or know ye in your might
And knowledge! My thoughts are not in this hour
Unworthy what I see, though my dust is;
Spirit! let me expire, or see them nearer.

LUCIFER - Art thou not nearer? look back to thine earth!

CAIN - Where is it? I see nothing save a mass
Of most innumerable lights.

LUCIFER - Look there!

CAIN - I cannot see it.

LUCIFER - Yet it sparkles still.

CAIN - That!—yonder!

LUCIFER - Yea.

CAIN - And wilt thou tell me so?
Why, I have seen the fire-flies and fire-worms
Sprinkle the dusky groves and the green banks
In the dim twilight, brighter than yon world
Which bears them.

LUCIFER - Thou hast seen both worms and worlds,
Each bright and sparkling—what dost think of them?

CAIN - That they are beautiful in their own sphere,
And that the night, which makes both beautiful,
The little shining fire-fly in its flight,
And the immortal star in its great course,
Must both be guided.

LUCIFER - But by whom or what?

CAIN - Show me.

LUCIFER - Dar'st thou behold?

CAIN - How know I what
I dare behold? As yet, thou hast shown nought
I dare not gaze on further.

LUCIFER - On, then, with me.
Wouldst thou behold things mortal or immortal?

CAIN - Why, what are things?

LUCIFER - Both partly: but what doth
Sit next thy heart?

CAIN - The things I see.

LUCIFER - But what
Sate nearest it?

CAIN - The things I have not seen,
Nor ever shall—the mysteries of Death.

LUCIFER - What, if I show to thee things which have died,
As I have shown thee much which cannot die?

CAIN - Do so.

LUCIFER - Away, then! on our mighty wings!

CAIN - Oh! how we cleave the blue! The stars fade from us!
The earth! where is my earth? Let me look on it,
For I was made of it.

LUCIFER - 'Tis now beyond thee,
Less, in the universe, than thou in it;
Yet deem not that thou canst escape it; thou
Shalt soon return to earth, and all its dust:
'Tis part of thy eternity, and mine.

CAIN - Where dost thou lead me?

LUCIFER - To what was before thee!
The phantasm of the world; of which thy world
Is but the wreck.

CAIN - What! is it not then new?

LUCIFER - No more than life is; and that was ere thou
Or I were, or the things which seem to us
Greater than either: many things will have

No end; and some, which would pretend to have
Had no beginning, have had one as mean
As thou; and mightier things have been extinct
To make way for much meaner than we can
Surmise; for moments only and the space
Have been and must be all unchangeable.
But changes make not death, except to clay;
But thou art clay—and canst but comprehend
That which was clay, and such thou shall behold.

CAIN - Clay—Spirit—what thou wilt—I can survey.

LUCIFER - Away, then!

CAIN - But the lights fade from me fast,
And some till now grew larger as we approached,
And wore the look of worlds.

LUCIFER - And such they are.

CAIN - And Edens in them?

LUCIFER - It may be.

CAIN - And men?

LUCIFER - Yea, or things higher.

CAIN - Aye! and serpents too?

LUCIFER - Wouldst thou have men without them? must no reptiles
Breathe, save the erect ones?

CAIN - How the lights recede!
Where fly we?

LUCIFER - To the world of phantoms, which
Are beings past, and shadows still to come.

CAIN - But it grows dark, and dark—the stars are gone!

LUCIFER - And yet thou seest.

CAIN - 'Tis a fearful light!
No sun—no moon—no lights innumerable—
The very blue of the empurpled night
Fades to a dreary twilight—yet I see
Huge dusky masses; but unlike the worlds
We were approaching, which, begirt with light,
Seemed full of life even when their atmosphere
Of light gave way, and showed them taking shapes

Unequal, of deep valleys and vast mountains;
And some emitting sparks, and some displaying
Enormous liquid plains, and some begirt
With luminous belts, and floating moons, which took,
Like them, the features of fair earth:—instead,
All here seems dark and dreadful.

LUCIFER - But distinct.
Thou seekest to behold Death, and dead things?

CAIN - I seek it not; but as I know there are
Such, and that my sire's sin makes him and me,
And all that we inherit, liable
To such, I would behold, at once, what I
Must one day see perforce.

LUCIFER - Behold!

CAIN - 'Tis darkness!

LUCIFER - And so it shall be ever—but we will
Unfold its gates!

CAIN - Enormous vapours roll
Apart—what's this?

LUCIFER - Enter!

CAIN - Can I return?

LUCIFER - Return! be sure: how else should Death be peopled?
Its present realm is thin to what it will be,
Through thee and thine.

CAIN - The clouds still open wide
And wider, and make widening circles round us!

LUCIFER - Advance!

CAIN - And thou!

LUCIFER - Fear not—without me thou
Couldst not have gone beyond thy world. On! on!

[They disappear through the clouds.

SCENE II. Hades.

Enter LUCIFER and CAIN.

CAIN - How silent and how vast are these dim worlds!
For they seem more than one, and yet more peopled
Than the huge brilliant luminous orbs which swung
So thickly in the upper air, that I
Had deemed them rather the bright populace
Of some all unimaginable Heaven,
Than things to be inhabited themselves,
But that on drawing near them I beheld
Their swelling into palpable immensity
Of matter, which seemed made for life to dwell on,
Rather than life itself. But here, all is
So shadowy, and so full of twilight, that
It speaks of a day past.

LUCIFER - It is the realm
Of Death.—Wouldst have it present?

CAIN - Till I know
That which it really is, I cannot answer.
But if it be as I have heard my father
Deal out in his long homilies, 'tis a thing—
Oh God! I dare not think on't! Curséd be
He who invented Life that leads to Death!
Or the dull mass of life, that, being life,
Could not retain, but needs must forfeit it—
Even for the innocent!

LUCIFER - Dost thou curse thy father?

CAIN - Cursed he not me in giving me my birth?
Cursed he not me before my birth, in daring
To pluck the fruit forbidden?

LUCIFER - Thou say'st well:
The curse is mutual 'twixt thy sire and thee—
But for thy sons and brother?

CAIN - Let them share it
With me, their sire and brother! What else is
Bequeathed to me? I leave them my inheritance!
Oh, ye interminable gloomy realms
Of swimming shadows and enormous shapes,
Some fully shown, some indistinct, and all
Mighty and melancholy—what are ye?
Live ye, or have ye lived?

LUCIFER - Somewhat of both.

CAIN - Then what is Death?

LUCIFER - What? Hath not he who made ye
Said 'tis another life?

CAIN - Till now he hath
Said nothing, save that all shall die.

LUCIFER - Perhaps
He one day will unfold that further secret.

CAIN - Happy the day!

LUCIFER - Yes; happy! when unfolded,
Through agonies unspeakable, and clogged
With agonies eternal, to innumerable
Yet unborn myriads of unconscious atoms,
All to be animated for this only!

CAIN - What are these mighty phantoms which I see
Floating around me?—They wear not the form
Of the Intelligences I have seen
Round our regretted and unentered Eden;
Nor wear the form of man as I have viewed it
In Adam's and in Abel's, and in mine,
Nor in my sister-bride's, nor in my children's:
And yet they have an aspect, which, though not
Of men nor angels, looks like something, which,
If not the last, rose higher than the first,
Haughty, and high, and beautiful, and full
Of seeming strength, but of inexplicable
Shape; for I never saw such. They bear not
The wing of Seraph, nor the face of man,
Nor form of mightiest brute, nor aught that is
Now breathing; mighty yet and beautiful
As the most beautiful and mighty which
Live, and yet so unlike them, that I scarce
Can call them living.

LUCIFER - Yet they lived.

CAIN - Where?

LUCIFER - Where
Thou livest.

CAIN - When?

LUCIFER - On what thou callest earth
They did inhabit.

CAIN - Adam is the first.

LUCIFER - Of thine, I grant thee—but too mean to be
The last of these.

CAIN - And what are they?

LUCIFER - That which
Thou shalt be.

CAIN - But what were they?

LUCIFER - Living, high,
Intelligent, good, great, and glorious things,
As much superior unto all thy sire
Adam could e'er have been in Eden, as
The sixty-thousandth generation shall be,
In its dull damp degeneracy, to
Thee and thy son;—and how weak they are, judge
By thy own flesh.

CAIN - Ah me! and did they perish?

LUCIFER - Yes, from their earth, as thou wilt fade from thine.

CAIN - But was mine theirs?

LUCIFER - It was.

CAIN - But not as now.
It is too little and too lowly to
Sustain such creatures.

LUCIFER - True, it was more glorious.

CAIN - And wherefore did it fall?

LUCIFER - Ask him who fells.

CAIN - But how?

LUCIFER - By a most crushing and inexorable
Destruction and disorder of the elements,
Which struck a world to chaos, as a chaos
Subsiding has struck out a world: such things,
Though rare in time, are frequent in eternity.—
Pass on, and gaze upon the past.

CAIN - 'Tis awful!

LUCIFER - And true. Behold these phantoms! they were once
Material as thou art.

CAIN - And must I be
Like them?

LUCIFER - Let He who made thee answer that.
I show thee what thy predecessors are,
And what they were thou feelest, in degree
Inferior as thy petty feelings and
Thy pettier portion of the immortal part
Of high intelligence and earthly strength.
What ye in common have with what they had
Is Life, and what ye shall have—Death: the rest
Of your poor attributes is such as suits
Reptiles engendered out of the subsiding
Slime of a mighty universe, crushed into
A scarcely-yet shaped planet, peopled with
Things whose enjoyment was to be in blindness—
A Paradise of Ignorance, from which
Knowledge was barred as poison. But behold
What these superior beings are or were;
Or, if it irk thee, turn thee back and till
The earth, thy task—I'll waft thee there in safety.

CAIN - No: I'll stay here.

LUCIFER - How long?

CAIN - For ever! Since
I must one day return here from the earth,
I rather would remain; I am sick of all
That dust has shown me—let me dwell in shadows.

LUCIFER - It cannot be: thou now beholdest as
A vision that which is reality.
To make thyself fit for this dwelling, thou
Must pass through what the things thou seest have passed—
The gates of Death.

CAIN - By what gate have we entered
Even now?

LUCIFER - By mine! But, plighted to return,
My spirit buoys thee up to breathe in regions
Where all is breathless save thyself. Gaze on;
But do not think to dwell here till thine hour
Is come!

CAIN - And these, too—can they ne'er repass
To earth again?

LUCIFER - Their earth is gone for ever—
So changed by its convulsion, they would not

Be conscious to a single present spot
Of its new scarcely hardened surface—'twas—
Oh, what a beautiful world it was!

CAIN -   And is!
It is not with the earth, though I must till it,
I feel at war—but that I may not profit
By what it bears of beautiful, untoiling,
Nor gratify my thousand swelling thoughts
With knowledge, nor allay my thousand fears
Of Death and Life.

LUCIFER - What thy world is, thou see'st,
But canst not comprehend the shadow of
That which it was.

CAIN - And those enormous creatures,
Phantoms inferior in intelligence
(At least so seeming) to the things we have passed,
Resembling somewhat the wild habitants
Of the deep woods of earth, the hugest which
Roar nightly in the forest, but ten-fold
In magnitude and terror; taller than
The cherub-guarded walls of Eden—with
Eyes flashing like the fiery swords which fence them—
And tusks projecting like the trees stripped of
Their bark and branches—what were they?

LUCIFER - That which
The Mammoth is in thy world;—but these lie
By myriads underneath its surface.

CAIN - But
None on it?

LUCIFER - No: for thy frail race to war
With them would render the curse on it useless—
'Twould be destroyed so early.

CAIN - But why war?

LUCIFER - You have forgotten the denunciation
Which drove your race from Eden—war with all things,
And death to all things, and disease to most things,
And pangs, and bitterness; these were the fruits
Of the forbidden tree.

CAIN - But animals—
Did they, too, eat of it, that they must die?

LUCIFER - Your Maker told ye, they were made for you,

As you for him.—You would not have their doom
Superior to your own? Had Adam not
Fallen, all had stood.

CAIN - Alas! the hopeless wretches!
They too must share my sire's fate, like his sons;
Like them, too, without having shared the apple;
Like them, too, without the so dear-bought knowledge!
It was a lying tree—for we know nothing.
At least it promised knowledge at the price
Of death—but knowledge still: but what knows man?

LUCIFER - It may be death leads to the highest knowledge;
And being of all things the sole thing certain,
At least leads to the surest science: therefore
The Tree was true, though deadly.

CAIN - These dim realms!
I see them, but I know them not.

LUCIFER - Because
Thy hour is yet afar, and matter cannot
Comprehend spirit wholly—but 'tis something
To know there are such realms.

CAIN - We knew already
That there was Death.

LUCIFER - But not what was beyond it.

CAIN - Nor know I now.

LUCIFER - Thou knowest that there is
A state, and many states beyond thine own—
And this thou knewest not this morn.

CAIN - But all
Seems dim and shadowy.

LUCIFER - Be content; it will
Seem clearer to thine immortality.

CAIN - And yon immeasurable liquid space
Of glorious azure which floats on beyond us,
Which looks like water, and which I should deem
The river which flows out of Paradise
Past my own dwelling, but that it is bankless
And boundless, and of an ethereal hue—
What is it?

LUCIFER - There is still some such on earth,

Although inferior, and thy children shall
Dwell near it—'tis the phantasm of an Ocean.

CAIN - 'Tis like another world; a liquid sun—
And those inordinate creatures sporting o'er
Its shining surface?

LUCIFER - Are its inhabitants,
The past Leviathans.

CAIN - And yon immense
Serpent, which rears his dripping mane and vasty
Head, ten times higher than the haughtiest cedar,
Forth from the abyss, looking as he could coil
Himself around the orbs we lately looked on—
Is he not of the kind which basked beneath
The Tree in Eden?

LUCIFER - Eve, thy mother, best
Can tell what shape of serpent tempted her.

CAIN - This seems too terrible. No doubt the other
Had more of beauty.

LUCIFER - Hast thou ne'er beheld him?

CAIN - Many of the same kind (at least so called)
But never that precisely, which persuaded
The fatal fruit, nor even of the same aspect.

LUCIFER - Your father saw him not?

CAIN - No: 'twas my mother
Who tempted him—she tempted by the serpent.

LUCIFER - Good man! whene'er thy wife, or thy sons' wives,
Tempt thee or them to aught that's new or strange,
Be sure thou seest first who hath tempted them!

CAIN - Thy precept comes too late: there is no more
For serpents to tempt woman to.

LUCIFER - But there
Are some things still which woman may tempt man to,
And man tempt woman:—let thy sons look to it!
My counsel is a kind one; for 'tis even
Given chiefly at my own expense; 'tis true,
'Twill not be followed, so there's little lost.

CAIN - I understand not this.

LUCIFER - The happier thou!—
Thy world and thou are still too young! Thou thinkest
Thyself most wicked and unhappy—is it
Not so?

CAIN - For crime, I know not; but for pain,
I have felt much.

LUCIFER - First-born of the first man!
Thy present state of sin—and thou art evil,
Of sorrow—and thou sufferest, are both Eden
In all its innocence compared to what
Thou shortly may'st be; and that state again,
In its redoubled wretchedness, a Paradise
To what thy sons' sons' sons, accumulating
In generations like to dust (which they
In fact but add to), shall endure and do.—
Now let us back to earth!

CAIN - And wherefore didst thou
Lead me here only to inform me this?

LUCIFER -Was not thy quest for knowledge?

CAIN - Yes—as being
The road to happiness!

LUCIFER - If truth be so,
Thou hast it.

CAIN - Then my father's God did well
When he prohibited the fatal Tree.

LUCIFER -But had done better in not planting it.
But ignorance of evil doth not save
From evil; it must still roll on the same,
A part of all things.

CAIN - Not of all things. No—
I'll not believe it—for I thirst for good.

LUCIFER - And who and what doth not? Who covets evil
For its own bitter sake?—None—nothing! 'tis
The leaven of all life, and lifelessness.

CAIN - Within those glorious orbs which we behold,
Distant, and dazzling, and innumerable,
Ere we came down into this phantom realm,
Ill cannot come: they are too beautiful.

LUCIFER - Thou hast seen them from afar.

CAIN - And what of that?
Distance can but diminish glory—they,
When nearer, must be more ineffable.

LUCIFER - Approach the things of earth most beautiful,
And judge their beauty near.

CAIN - I have done this—
The loveliest thing I know is loveliest nearest.

LUCIFER - Then there must be delusion.—What is that
Which being nearest to thine eyes is still
More beautiful than beauteous things remote?

CAIN - My sister Adah.—All the stars of heaven,
The deep blue noon of night, lit by an orb
Which looks a spirit, or a spirit's world—
The hues of twilight—the Sun's gorgeous coming—
His setting indescribable, which fills
My eyes with pleasant tears as I behold
Him sink, and feel my heart float softly with him
Along that western paradise of clouds—
The forest shade, the green bough, the bird's voice—
The vesper bird's, which seems to sing of love,
And mingles with the song of Cherubim,
As the day closes over Eden's walls;—
All these are nothing, to my eyes and heart,
Like Adah's face: I turn from earth and heaven
To gaze on it.

LUCIFER - 'Tis fair as frail mortality,
In the first dawn and bloom of young creation,
And earliest embraces of earth's parents,
Can make its offspring; still it is delusion.

CAIN - You think so, being not her brother.

LUCIFER - Mortal!
My brotherhood's with those who have no children.

CAIN - Then thou canst have no fellowship with us.

LUCIFER - It may be that thine own shall be for me.
But if thou dost possess a beautiful
Being beyond all beauty in thine eyes,
Why art thou wretched?

CAIN - Why do I exist?
Why art thou wretched? why are all things so?
Ev'n he who made us must be, as the maker

Of things unhappy! To produce destruction
Can surely never be the task of joy,
And yet my sire says he's omnipotent:
Then why is Evil—he being Good? I asked
This question of my father; and he said,
Because this Evil only was the path
To Good. Strange Good, that must arise from out
Its deadly opposite. I lately saw
A lamb stung by a reptile: the poor suckling
Lay foaming on the earth, beneath the vain
And piteous bleating of its restless dam;
My father plucked some herbs, and laid them to
The wound; and by degrees the helpless wretch
Resumed its careless life, and rose to drain
The mother's milk, who o'er it tremulous
Stood licking its reviving limbs with joy.
Behold, my son! said Adam, how from Evil
Springs Good!

LUCIFER - What didst thou answer?

CAIN - Nothing; for
He is my father: but I thought, that 'twere
A better portion for the animal
Never to have been stung at all, than to
Purchase renewal of its little life
With agonies unutterable, though
Dispelled by antidotes.

LUCIFER - But as thou saidst
Of all belovéd things thou lovest her
Who shared thy mother's milk, and giveth hers
Unto thy children—

CAIN - Most assuredly:
What should I be without her?

LUCIFER - What am I?

CAIN - Dost thou love nothing?

LUCIFER - What does thy God love?

CAIN - All things, my father says; but I confess
I see it not in their allotment here.

LUCIFER - And, therefore, thou canst not see if I love
Or no—except some vast and general purpose,
To which particular things must melt like snows.

CAIN - Snows! what are they?

LUCIFER - Be happier in not knowing
What thy remoter offspring must encounter;
But bask beneath the clime which knows no winter.

CAIN - But dost thou not love something like thyself?

LUCIFER - And dost thou love thyself?

CAIN - Yes, but love more
What makes my feelings more endurable,
And is more than myself, because I love it!

LUCIFER - Thou lovest it, because 'tis beautiful,
As was the apple in thy mother's eye;
And when it ceases to be so, thy love
Will cease, like any other appetite.

CAIN - Cease to be beautiful! how can that be?

LUCIFER - With time.

CAIN - But time has passed, and hitherto
Even Adam and my mother both are fair:
Not fair like Adah and the Seraphim—
But very fair.

LUCIFER - All that must pass away
In them and her.

CAIN - I'm sorry for it; but
Cannot conceive my love for her the less:
And when her beauty disappears, methinks
He who creates all beauty will lose more
Than me in seeing perish such a work.

LUCIFER - I pity thee who lovest what must perish.

CAIN - And I thee who lov'st nothing.

LUCIFER - And thy brother—
Sits he not near thy heart?

CAIN - Why should he not?

LUCIFER - Thy father loves him well—so does thy God.

CAIN - And so do I.

LUCIFER - 'Tis well and meekly done.

CAIN - Meekly!

LUCIFER - He is the second born of flesh,
And is his mother's favourite.

CAIN - Let him keep
Her favour, since the Serpent was the first
To win it.

LUCIFER - And his father's?

CAIN - What is that
To me? should I not love that which all love?

LUCIFER - And the Jehovah—the indulgent Lord,
And bounteous planter of barred Paradise—
He, too, looks smilingly on Abel.

CAIN - I
Ne'er saw him, and I know not if he smiles.

LUCIFER - But you have seen his angels.

CAIN - Rarely.

LUCIFER - But
Sufficiently to see they love your brother:
His sacrifices are acceptable.

CAIN - So be they! wherefore speak to me of this?

LUCIFER - Because thou hast thought of this ere now.

CAIN - And if
I have thought, why recall a thought that—
(he pauses as agitated)—Spirit!
Here we are in thy world; speak not of mine.
Thou hast shown me wonders: thou hast shown me those
Mighty Pre-Adamites who walked the earth
Of which ours is the wreck: thou hast pointed out
Myriads of starry worlds, of which our own
Is the dim and remote companion, in
Infinity of life: thou hast shown me shadows
Of that existence with the dreaded name
Which my sire brought us—Death; thou hast shown me much
But not all: show me where Jehovah dwells,
In his especial Paradise—or thine:
Where is it?

LUCIFER - Here, and o'er all space.

CAIN - But ye
Have some allotted dwelling—as all things;
Clay has its earth, and other worlds their tenants;
All temporary breathing creatures their
Peculiar element; and things which have
Long ceased to breathe our breath, have theirs, thou say'st;
And the Jehovah and thyself have thine—
Ye do not dwell together?

LUCIFER - No, we reign
Together; but our dwellings are asunder.

CAIN - Would there were only one of ye! perchance
An unity of purpose might make union
In elements which seem now jarred in storms.
How came ye, being Spirits wise and infinite,
To separate? Are ye not as brethren in
Your essence—and your nature, and your glory?

LUCIFER - Art not thou Abel's brother?

CAIN - We are brethren,
And so we shall remain; but were it not so,
Is spirit like to flesh? can it fall out—
Infinity with Immortality?
Jarring and turning space to misery—
For what?

LUCIFER - To reign.

CAIN - Did ye not tell me that
Ye are both eternal?

LUCIFER - Yea!

CAIN - And what I have seen—
Yon blue immensity, is boundless?

LUCIFER - Aye.
CAIN - And cannot ye both reign, then?—is there not
Enough?—why should ye differ?

LUCIFER - We both reign.

CAIN - But one of you makes evil.

LUCIFER - Which?

CAIN - Thou! for
If thou canst do man good, why dost thou not?

LUCIFER - And why not he who made? I made ye not;
Ye are his creatures, and not mine.

CAIN - Then leave us
His creatures, as thou say'st we are, or show me
Thy dwelling, or his dwelling.

LUCIFER - I could show thee
Both; but the time will come thou shalt see one
Of them for evermore.

CAIN - And why not now?

LUCIFER - Thy human mind hath scarcely grasp to gather
The little I have shown thee into calm
And clear thought: and thou wouldst go on aspiring
To the great double Mysteries! the two Principles!
And gaze upon them on their secret thrones!
Dust! limit thy ambition; for to see
Either of these would be for thee to perish!

CAIN - And let me perish, so I see them!

LUCIFER - There
The son of her who snatched the apple spake!
But thou wouldst only perish, and not see them;
That sight is for the other state.

CAIN - Of Death?

LUCIFER - That is the prelude.

CAIN - Then I dread it less,
Now that I know it leads to something definite.

LUCIFER - And now I will convey thee to thy world,
Where thou shall multiply the race of Adam,
Eat, drink, toil, tremble, laugh, weep, sleep—and die!

CAIN - And to what end have I beheld these things
Which thou hast shown me?

LUCIFER - Didst thou not require
Knowledge? And have I not, in what I showed,
Taught thee to know thyself?

CAIN - Alas! I seem
Nothing.

LUCIFER - And this should be the human sum

Of knowledge, to know mortal nature's nothingness;
Bequeath that science to thy children, and
'Twill spare them many tortures.

CAIN - Haughty spirit!
Thou speak'st it proudly; but thyself, though proud,
Hast a superior.

LUCIFER - No! By heaven, which he
Holds, and the abyss, and the immensity
Of worlds and life, which I hold with him—No!
I have a Victor—true; but no superior.
Homage he has from all—but none from me:
I battle it against him, as I battled
In highest Heaven—through all Eternity,
And the unfathomable gulfs of Hades,
And the interminable realms of space,
And the infinity of endless ages,
All, all, will I dispute! And world by world,
And star by star, and universe by universe,
Shall tremble in the balance, till the great
Conflict shall cease, if ever it shall cease,
Which it ne'er shall, till he or I be quenched!
And what can quench our immortality,
Or mutual and irrevocable hate?
He as a conqueror will call the conquered
Evil; but what will be the Good he gives?
Were I the victor, his works would be deemed
The only evil ones. And you, ye new
And scarce-born mortals, what have been his gifts
To you already, in your little world?

CAIN - But few; and some of those but bitter.

LUCIFER - Back
With me, then, to thine earth, and try the rest
Of his celestial boons to you and yours.
Evil and Good are things in their own essence,
And not made good or evil by the Giver;
But if he gives you good—so call him; if
Evil springs from him, do not name it mine,
Till ye know better its true fount; and judge
Not by words, though of Spirits, but the fruits
Of your existence, such as it must be.
One good gift has the fatal apple given,—
Your reason:—let it not be overswayed
By tyrannous threats to force you into faith
'Gainst all external sense and inward feeling:
Think and endure,—and form an inner world
In your own bosom—where the outward fails;
So shall you nearer be the spiritual

Nature, and war triumphant with your own.

[They disappear.

SCENE I. The Earth, near Eden, as in Act I.

Enter CAIN and ADAH.

ADAH - Hush! tread softly, Cain!

CAIN - I will—but wherefore?

ADAH - Our little Enoch sleeps upon yon bed
Of leaves, beneath the cypress.

CAIN - Cypress! 'tis
A gloomy tree, which looks as if it mourned
O'er what it shadows; wherefore didst thou choose it
For our child's canopy?

ADAH - Because its branches
Shut out the sun like night, and therefore seemed
Fitting to shadow slumber.

CAIN - Aye, the last—
And longest; but no matter—lead me to him.
[They go up to the child.
How lovely he appears! his little cheeks,
In their pure incarnation, vying with
The rose leaves strewn beneath them.

ADAH - And his lips, too,
How beautifully parted! No; you shall not
Kiss him, at least not now: he will awake soon—
His hour of mid-day rest is nearly over;
But it were pity to disturb him till
'Tis closed.

CAIN - You have said well; I will contain
My heart till then. He smiles, and sleeps!—sleep on,
And smile, thou little, young inheritor
Of a world scarce less young: sleep on, and smile!
Thine are the hours and days when both are cheering
And innocent! thou hast not plucked the fruit—
Thou know'st not thou art naked! Must the time
Come thou shalt be amerced for sins unknown,

Which were not thine nor mine? But now sleep on!
His cheeks are reddening into deeper smiles,
And shining lids are trembling o'er his long
Lashes, dark as the cypress which waves o'er them;
Half open, from beneath them the clear blue
Laughs out, although in slumber. He must dream—
Of what? Of Paradise!—Aye! dream of it,
My disinherited boy! 'Tis but a dream;
For never more thyself, thy sons, nor fathers,
Shall walk in that forbidden place of joy!

ADAH - Dear Cain! Nay, do not whisper o'er our son
Such melancholy yearnings o'er the past:
Why wilt thou always mourn for Paradise?
Can we not make another?

CAIN - Where?

ADAH - Here, or
Where'er thou wilt: where'er thou art, I feel not
The want of this so much regretted Eden.
Have I not thee—our boy—our sire, and brother,
And Zillah—our sweet sister, and our Eve,
To whom we owe so much besides our birth?

CAIN - Yes—Death, too, is amongst the debts we owe her.

ADAH - Cain! that proud Spirit, who withdrew thee hence,
Hath saddened thine still deeper. I had hoped
The promised wonders which thou hast beheld,
Visions, thou say'st, of past and present worlds,
Would have composed thy mind into the calm
Of a contented knowledge; but I see
Thy guide hath done thee evil: still I thank him,
And can forgive him all, that he so soon
Hath given thee back to us.

CAIN - So soon?

ADAH - 'Tis scarcely
Two hours since ye departed: two long hours
To me, but only hours upon the sun.

CAIN - And yet I have approached that sun, and seen
Worlds which he once shone on, and never more
Shall light; and worlds he never lit: methought
Years had rolled o'er my absence.

ADAH - Hardly hours.

CAIN - The mind then hath capacity of time,

And measures it by that which it beholds,
Pleasing or painful; little or almighty.
I had beheld the immemorial works
Of endless beings; skirred extinguished worlds;
And, gazing on eternity, methought
I had borrowed more by a few drops of ages
From its immensity: but now I feel
My littleness again. Well said the Spirit,
That I was nothing!

ADAH - Wherefore said he so?
Jehovah said not that.

CAIN - No: he contents him
With making us the nothing which we are;
And after flattering dust with glimpses of
Eden and Immortality, resolves
It back to dust again—for what?

ADAH - Thou know'st—
Even for our parents' error.

CAIN - What is that
To us? they sinned, then let them die!

ADAH - Thou hast not spoken well, nor is that thought
Thy own, but of the Spirit who was with thee.
Would I could die for them, so they might live!

CAIN - Why, so say I—provided that one victim
Might satiate the Insatiable of life,
And that our little rosy sleeper there
Might never taste of death nor human sorrow,
Nor hand it down to those who spring from him.

ADAH - How know we that some such atonement one day
May not redeem our race?

CAIN - By sacrificing
The harmless for the guilty? what atonement
Were there? why, we are innocent: what have we
Done, that we must be victims for a deed
Before our birth, or need have victims to
Atone for this mysterious, nameless sin—
If it be such a sin to seek for knowledge?

ADAH - Alas! thou sinnest now, my Cain: thy words
Sound impious in mine ears.

CAIN - Then leave me!

ADAH - Never,
Though thy God left thee.

CAIN - Say, what have we here?

ADAH - Two altars, which our brother Abel made
During thine absence, whereupon to offer
A sacrifice to God on thy return.

CAIN - And how knew he, that I would be so ready
With the burnt offerings, which he daily brings
With a meek brow, whose base humility
Shows more of fear than worship—as a bribe
To the Creator?

ADAH - Surely, 'tis well done.

CAIN - One altar may suffice; I have no offering.

ADAH - The fruits of the earth, the early, beautiful,
Blossom and bud—and bloom of flowers and fruits—
These are a goodly offering to the Lord,
Given with a gentle and a contrite spirit.

CAIN - I have toiled, and tilled, and sweaten in the sun,
According to the curse:—must I do more?
For what should I be gentle? for a war
With all the elements ere they will yield
The bread we eat? For what must I be grateful?
For being dust, and grovelling in the dust,
Till I return to dust? If I am nothing—
For nothing shall I be an hypocrite,
And seem well-pleased with pain? For what should I
Be contrite? for my father's sin, already
Expiate with what we all have undergone,
And to be more than expiated by
The ages prophesied, upon our seed.
Little deems our young blooming sleeper, there,
The germs of an eternal misery
To myriads is within him! better 'twere
I snatched him in his sleep, and dashed him 'gainst
The rocks, than let him live to—

ADAH - Oh, my God!
Touch not the child—my child! thy child! Oh, Cain!

CAIN - Fear not! for all the stars, and all the power
Which sways them, I would not accost yon infant
With ruder greeting than a father's kiss.

ADAH - Then, why so awful in thy speech?

CAIN - I said,
'Twere better that he ceased to live, than give
Life to so much of sorrow as he must
Endure, and, harder still, bequeath; but since
That saying jars you, let us only say—
'Twere better that he never had been born.

ADAH - Oh, do not say so! Where were then the joys,
The mother's joys of watching, nourishing,
And loving him? Soft! he awakes. Sweet Enoch!

[She goes to the child.

Oh, Cain! look on him; see how full of life,
Of strength, of bloom, of beauty, and of joy—
How like to me—how like to thee, when gentle—
For then we are all alike; is't not so, Cain?
Mother, and sire, and son, our features are
Reflected in each other; as they are
In the clear waters, when they are gentle, and
When thou art gentle. Love us, then, my Cain!
And love thyself for our sakes, for we love thee.
Look! how he laughs and stretches out his arms,
And opens wide his blue eyes upon thine,
To hail his father; while his little form
Flutters as winged with joy. Talk not of pain!
The childless cherubs well might envy thee
The pleasures of a parent! Bless him, Cain!
As yet he hath no words to thank thee, but
His heart will, and thine own too.

CAIN - Bless thee, boy!
If that a mortal blessing may avail thee,
To save thee from the Serpent's curse!

ADAH - It shall.
Surely a father's blessing may avert
A reptile's subtlety.

CAIN - Of that I doubt;
But bless him ne'er the less.

ADAH - Our brother comes.

CAIN - Thy brother Abel.

Enter ABEL.

ABEL - Welcome, Cain! My brother,
The peace of God be on thee!

CAIN - Abel, hail!

ABEL - Our sister tells me that thou hast been wandering,
In high communion with a Spirit, far
Beyond our wonted range. Was he of those
We have seen and spoken with, like to our father?

CAIN - No.

ABEL - Why then commune with him? he may be
A foe to the Most High.

CAIN - And friend to man.
Has the Most High been so—if so you term him?

ABEL - Term him! your words are strange to-day, my brother.
My sister Adah, leave us for awhile—
We mean to sacrifice.

ADAH - Farewell, my Cain;
But first embrace thy son. May his soft spirit,
And Abel's pious ministry, recall thee
To peace and holiness!

[Exit ADAH, with her child.

ABEL - Where hast thou been?

CAIN - I know not.

ABEL - Nor what thou hast seen?

CAIN - The dead—
The Immortal—the Unbounded—the Omnipotent—
The overpowering mysteries of space—
The innumerable worlds that were and are—
A whirlwind of such overwhelming things,
Suns, moons, and earths, upon their loud-voiced spheres
Singing in thunder round me, as have made me
Unfit for mortal converse: leave me, Abel.

ABEL - Thine eyes are flashing with unnatural light—
Thy cheek is flushed with an unnatural hue—
Thy words are fraught with an unnatural sound—
What may this mean?

CAIN - It means—I pray thee, leave me.

ABEL - Not till we have prayed and sacrificed together.

CAIN - Abel, I pray thee, sacrifice alone—
Jehovah loves thee well.

ABEL - Both well, I hope.

CAIN - But thee the better: I care not for that;
Thou art fitter for his worship than I am;
Revere him, then—but let it be alone—
At least, without me.

ABEL - Brother, I should ill
Deserve the name of our great father's son,
If, as my elder, I revered thee not,
And in the worship of our God, called not
On thee to join me, and precede me in
Our priesthood—'tis thy place.

CAIN - But I have ne'er
Asserted it.

ABEL - The more my grief; I pray thee
To do so now: thy soul seems labouring in
Some strong delusion; it will calm thee.

CAIN - No;
Nothing can calm me more. Calm! say I? Never
Knew I what calm was in the soul, although
I have seen the elements stilled. My Abel, leave me!
Or let me leave thee to thy pious purpose.

ABEL - Neither; we must perform our task together.
Spurn me not.

CAIN - If it must be so—well, then,
What shall I do?

ABEL - Choose one of those two altars.

CAIN - Choose for me: they to me are so much turf
And stone.

ABEL - Choose thou!

CAIN - I have chosen.

ABEL - 'Tis the highest,
And suits thee, as the elder. Now prepare
Thine offerings.

CAIN - Where are thine?

ABEL - Behold them here—
The firstlings of the flock, and fat thereof—
A shepherd's humble offering.

CAIN - I have no flocks;
I am a tiller of the ground, and must
Yield what it yieldeth to my toil—its fruit:

[He gathers fruits.

Behold them in their various bloom and ripeness.

[They dress their altars, and kindle aflame upon them.

ABEL - My brother, as the elder, offer first
Thy prayer and thanksgiving with sacrifice.

CAIN - No—I am new to this; lead thou the way,
And I will follow—as I may.

ABEL - (kneeling) Oh, God!
Who made us, and who breathed the breath of life
Within our nostrils, who hath blessed us,
And spared, despite our father's sin, to make
His children all lost, as they might have been,
Had not thy justice been so tempered with
The mercy which is thy delight, as to
Accord a pardon like a Paradise,
Compared with our great crimes:—Sole Lord of light!
Of good, and glory, and eternity!
Without whom all were evil, and with whom
Nothing can err, except to some good end
Of thine omnipotent benevolence!
Inscrutable, but still to be fulfilled!
Accept from out thy humble first of shepherds'
First of the first-born flocks—an offering,
In itself nothing—as what offering can be
Aught unto thee?—but yet accept it for
The thanksgiving of him who spreads it in
The face of thy high heaven—bowing his own
Even to the dust, of which he is—in honour
Of thee, and of thy name, for evermore!

CAIN - (standing erect during this speech).
Spirit whate'er or whosoe'er thou art,
Omnipotent, it may be—and, if good,
Shown in the exemption of thy deeds from evil;
Jehovah upon earth! and God in heaven!
And it may be with other names, because
Thine attributes seem many, as thy works:—
If thou must be propitiated with prayers,

Take them! If thou must be induced with altars,
And softened with a sacrifice, receive them;
Two beings here erect them unto thee.
If thou lov'st blood, the shepherd's shrine, which smokes
On my right hand, hath shed it for thy service
In the first of his flock, whose limbs now reek
In sanguinary incense to thy skies;
Or, if the sweet and blooming fruits of earth,
And milder seasons, which the unstained turf
I spread them on now offers in the face
Of the broad sun which ripened them, may seem
Good to thee—inasmuch as they have not
Suffered in limb or life—and rather form
A sample of thy works, than supplication
To look on ours! If a shrine without victim,
And altar without gore, may win thy favour,
Look on it! and for him who dresseth it,
He is—such as thou mad'st him; and seeks nothing
Which must be won by kneeling: if he's evil,
Strike him! thou art omnipotent, and may'st—
For what can he oppose? If he be good,
Strike him, or spare him, as thou wilt! since all
Rests upon thee; and Good and Evil seem
To have no power themselves, save in thy will—
And whether that be good or ill I know not,
Not being omnipotent, nor fit to judge
Omnipotence—but merely to endure
Its mandate; which thus far I have endured.

[The fire upon the altar of ABEL kindles into a column of the brightest flame, and ascends to heaven;
while a whirlwind throws down the altar of CAIN, and scatters the fruits abroad upon the earths.

ABEL - (kneeling) Oh, brother, pray! Jehovah's wroth with thee.

CAIN - Why so?

ABEL - Thy fruits are scattered on the earth.

CAIN - From earth they came, to earth let them return;
Their seed will bear fresh fruit there ere the summer:
Thy burnt flesh-offering prospers better; see
How Heaven licks up the flames, when thick with blood!

ABEL -Think not upon my offering's acceptance,
But make another of thine own—before
It is too late.

CAIN - I will build no more altars,
Nor suffer any—

ABEL - (rising) Cain! what meanest thou?

CAIN - To cast down yon vile flatterer of the clouds,
The smoky harbinger of thy dull prayers—
Thine altar, with its blood of lambs and kids,
Which fed on milk, to be destroyed in blood.

ABEL - (opposing him).
Thou shalt not:—add not impious works to impious
Words! let that altar stand—'tis hallowed now
By the immortal pleasure of Jehovah,
In his acceptance of the victims.

CAIN - His!
His pleasure! what was his high pleasure in
The fumes of scorching flesh and smoking blood,
To the pain of the bleating mothers, which
Still yearn for their dead offspring? or the pangs
Of the sad ignorant victims underneath
Thy pious knife? Give way! this bloody record
Shall not stand in the sun, to shame creation!

ABEL - Brother, give back! thou shalt not touch my altar
With violence: if that thou wilt adopt it,
To try another sacrifice, 'tis thine.

CAIN - Another sacrifice! Give way, or else
That sacrifice may be—

ABEL - What mean'st thou?

CAIN - Give—
Give way!—thy God loves blood!—then look to it:—
Give way, ere he hath more!

ABEL - In his great name,
I stand between thee and the shrine which hath
Had his acceptance.

CAIN - If thou lov'st thyself,
Stand back till I have strewed this turf along
Its native soil:—else—

ABEL - (opposing him) I love God far more
Than life.

CAIN - (striking him with a brand, on the temples, which he snatches from the altar).
Then take thy life unto thy God,
Since he loves lives.

ABEL - (falls). What hast thou done—my brother?

CAIN - Brother!

ABEL - Oh, God! receive thy servant! and
Forgive his slayer, for he knew not what
He did—Cain, give me—give me thy hand; and tell
Poor Zillah—

CAIN - (after a moment's stupefaction)
My hand! 'tis all red, and with—
What?

[A long pause.—Looking slowly round.

Where am I? alone! Where's Abel? where
Cain? Can it be that I am he? My brother,
Awake!—why liest thou so long on the green earth?
'Tis not the hour of slumber:—why so pale?
What hast thou!—thou wert full of life this morn!
Abel! I pray thee, mock me not! I smote
Too fiercely, but not fatally. Ah, why
Wouldst thou oppose me? This is mockery;
And only done to daunt me:—'twas a blow—
And but a blow. Stir—stir—nay, only stir!
Why, so—that's well!—thou breathest! breathe upon me!
Oh God! Oh God!

ABEL - (very faintly) What's he who speaks of God?

CAIN - Thy murderer.

ABEL - Then may God forgive him! Cain,
Comfort poor Zillah:—she has but one brother
Now.

[ABEL dies.

CAIN - And I none!—Who makes me brotherless?
His eyes are open! then he is not dead!
Death is like sleep; and sleep shuts down our lids.
His lips, too, are apart; why then he breathes;
And yet I feel it not.—His heart!—his heart!—
Let me see, doth it beat? methinks—No!—no!
This is a vision, else I am become
The native of another and worse world.
The earth swims round me:—what is this?—'tis wet;

[Puts his hand to his brow, and then looks at it.

And yet there are no dews! 'Tis blood—my blood—
My brother's and my own! and shed by me!
Then what have I further to do with life,

Since I have taken life from my own flesh?
But he can not be dead!—Is silence death?
No; he will wake; then let me watch by him.
Life cannot be so slight, as to be quenched
Thus quickly!—he hath spoken to me since—
What shall I say to him?—My brother!—No:
He will not answer to that name; for brethren
Smite not each other. Yet—yet—speak to me.
Oh! for a word more of that gentle voice,
That I may bear to hear my own again!

Enter ZILLAH.

ZILLAH - I heard a heavy sound; what can it be?
'Tis Cain; and watching by my husband. What
Dost thou there, brother? Doth he sleep? Oh, Heaven!
What means this paleness, and yon stream?—No, no!
It is not blood; for who would shed his blood?
Abel! what's this?—who hath done this? He moves not;
He breathes not: and his hands drop down from mine
With stony lifelessness! Ah! cruel Cain!
Why camest thou not in time to save him from
This violence? Whatever hath assailed him,
Thou wert the stronger, and shouldst have stepped in
Between him and aggression! Father!—Eve!—
Adah!—come hither! Death is in the world!
[Exit ZILLAH, calling on her Parents, etc.

CAIN - (solus). And who hath brought him there?—I—who abhor
The name of Death so deeply, that the thought
Empoisoned all my life, before I knew
His aspect—I have led him here, and given
My brother to his cold and still embrace,
As if he would not have asserted his
Inexorable claim without my aid.
I am awake at last—a dreary dream
Had maddened me;—but he shall ne'er awake!

Enter ADAM, EVE, ADAH, and ZILLAH.

ADAM - A voice of woe from Zillah brings me here—
What do I see?—'Tis true!—My son!—my son!
Woman, behold the Serpent's work, and thine!   [To EVE.

EVE - Oh! speak not of it now: the Serpent's fangs
Are in my heart! My best beloved, Abel!
Jehovah! this is punishment beyond
A mother's sin, to take him from me!

ADAM - Who,
Or what hath done this deed?—speak, Cain, since thou

Wert present; was it some more hostile angel,
Who walks not with Jehovah? or some wild
Brute of the forest?

EVE - Ah! a livid light
Breaks through, as from a thunder-cloud! yon brand
Massy and bloody! snatched from off the altar,
And black with smoke, and red with—

ADAM - Speak, my son!
Speak, and assure us, wretched as we are,
That we are not more miserable still.

ADAH - Speak, Cain! and say it was not thou!

EVE - It was!
I see it now—he hangs his guilty head,
And covers his ferocious eye with hands
Incarnadine!

ADAH - Mother, thou dost him wrong—
Cain! clear thee from this horrible accusal,
Which grief wrings from our parent.

EVE - Hear, Jehovah!
May the eternal Serpent's curse be on him!
For he was fitter for his seed than ours.
May all his days be desolate! May—

ADAH - Hold!
Curse him not, mother, for he is thy son—
Curse him not, mother, for he is my brother,
And my betrothed.

EVE - He hath left thee no brother—
Zillah no husband—me no son! for thus
I curse him from my sight for evermore!
All bonds I break between us, as he broke
That of his nature, in yon—Oh Death! Death!
Why didst thou not take me, who first incurred thee?
Why dost thou not so now?

ADAM - Eve! let not this,
Thy natural grief, lead to impiety!
A heavy doom was long forespoken to us;
And now that it begins, let it be borne
In such sort as may show our God, that we
Are faithful servants to his holy will.

EVE - (pointing to CAIN)
His will! the will of yon Incarnate Spirit

Of Death, whom I have brought upon the earth
To strew it with the dead. May all the curses
Of life be on him! and his agonies
Drive him forth o'er the wilderness, like us
From Eden, till his children do by him
As he did by his brother! May the swords
And wings of fiery Cherubim pursue him
By day and night—snakes spring up in his path—
Earth's fruits be ashes in his mouth—the leaves
On which he lays his head to sleep be strewed
With scorpions! May his dreams be of his victim!
His waking a continual dread of Death!
May the clear rivers turn to blood as he
Stoops down to stain them with his raging lip!
May every element shun or change to him!
May he live in the pangs which others die with!
And Death itself wax something worse than Death
To him who first acquainted him with man!
Hence, fratricide! henceforth that word is Cain,
Through all the coming myriads of mankind,
Who shall abhor thee, though thou wert their sire!
May the grass wither from thy feet! the woods
Deny thee shelter! earth a home! the dust
A grave! the sun his light! and heaven her God!

[Exit EVE.

ADAM - Cain! get thee forth: we dwell no more together.
Depart! and leave the dead to me—I am
Henceforth alone—we never must meet more.

ADAH - Oh, part not with him thus, my father: do not
Add thy deep curse to Eve's upon his head!

ADAM - I curse him not: his spirit be his curse.
Come, Zillah!

ZILLAH - I must watch my husband's corse.

ADAM - We will return again, when he is gone
Who hath provided for us this dread office.
Come, Zillah!

ZILLAH - Yet one kiss on yon pale clay,
And those lips once so warm—my heart! my heart!

[Exeunt ADAM and ZILLAH weeping.

ADAH - Cain! thou hast heard, we must go forth. I am ready,
So shall our children be. I will bear Enoch,
And you his sister. Ere the sun declines

Let us depart, nor walk the wilderness
Under the cloud of night.—Nay, speak to me.
To me—thine own.

CAIN - Leave me!

ADAH - Why, all have left thee.

CAIN - And wherefore lingerest thou? Dost thou not fear
To dwell with one who hath done this?

ADAH - I fear
Nothing except to leave thee, much as I
Shrink from the deed which leaves thee brotherless.
I must not speak of this—it is between thee
And the great God.

A VOICE from within exclaims - Cain! Cain!

ADAH - Hear'st thou that voice?

The VOICE within - Cain! Cain!

ADAH - It soundeth like an angel's tone.

Enter the ANGEL of the Lord.

ANGEL - Where is thy brother Abel?

CAIN - Am I then
My brother's keeper?

ANGEL - Cain! what hast thou done?
The voice of thy slain brother's blood cries out,
Even from the ground, unto the Lord!—Now art thou
Cursed from the earth, which opened late her mouth
To drink thy brother's blood from thy rash hand.
Henceforth, when thou shalt till the ground, it shall not
Yield thee her strength; a fugitive shalt thou
Be from this day, and vagabond on earth!

ADAH - This punishment is more than he can bear.
Behold thou drivest him from the face of earth,
And from the face of God shall he be hid.
A fugitive and vagabond on earth,
'Twill come to pass, that whoso findeth him
Shall slay him.

CAIN - Would they could! but who are they
Shall slay me? Where are these on the lone earth
As yet unpeopled?

ANGEL - Thou hast slain thy brother,
And who shall warrant thee against thy son?

ADAH - Angel of Light! be merciful, nor say
That this poor aching breast now nourishes
A murderer in my boy, and of his father.

ANGEL - Then he would but be what his father is.
Did not the milk of Eve give nutriment
To him thou now seest so besmeared with blood?
The fratricide might well engender parricides.—
But it shall not be so—the Lord thy God
And mine commandeth me to set his seal
On Cain, so that he may go forth in safety.
Who slayeth Cain, a sevenfold vengeance shall
Be taken on his head. Come hither!

CAIN - What
Wouldst thou with me?

ANGEL - To mark upon thy brow
Exemption from such deeds as thou hast done.

CAIN - No, let me die!

ANGEL - It must not be.

[The ANGEL sets the mark on CAIN'S brow.

CAIN - It burns
My brow, but nought to that which is within it!
Is there more? let me meet it as I may.

ANGEL - Stern hast thou been and stubborn from the womb,
As the ground thou must henceforth till; but he
Thou slew'st was gentle as the flocks he tended.

CAIN - After the fall too soon was I begotten;
Ere yet my mother's mind subsided from
The Serpent, and my sire still mourned for Eden.
That which I am, I am; I did not seek
For life, nor did I make myself; but could I
With my own death redeem him from the dust—
And why not so? let him return to day,
And I lie ghastly! so shall be restored
By God the life to him he loved; and taken
From me a being I ne'er loved to bear.

ANGEL - Who shall heal murder? what is done, is done;
Go forth! fulfil thy days! and be thy deeds

Unlike the last!

[The ANGEL disappears.

ADAH - He's gone, let us go forth;
I hear our little Enoch cry within
Our bower.

CAIN - Ah! little knows he what he weeps for!
And I who have shed blood cannot shed tears!
But the four rivers would not cleanse my soul.
Think'st thou my boy will bear to look on me?

ADAH - If I thought that he would not, I would—

CAIN - (interrupting her) No,
No more of threats: we have had too many of them:
Go to our children—I will follow thee.

ADAH - I will not leave thee lonely with the dead—
Let us depart together.

CAIN - Oh! thou dead
And everlasting witness! whose unsinking
Blood darkens earth and heaven! what thou now art
I know not! but if thou seest what I am,
I think thou wilt forgive him, whom his God
Can ne'er forgive, nor his own soul.—Farewell!
I must not, dare not touch what I have made thee.
I, who sprung from the same womb with thee, drained
The same breast, clasped thee often to my own,
In fondness brotherly and boyish, I
Can never meet thee more, nor even dare
To do that for thee, which thou shouldst have done
For me—compose thy limbs into their grave—
The first grave yet dug for mortality.
But who hath dug that grave? Oh, earth! Oh, earth!
For all the fruits thou hast rendered to me, I
Give thee back this.—Now for the wilderness!

[ADAH stoops down and kisses the body of ABEL.

ADAH - A dreary, and an early doom, my brother,
Has been thy lot! Of all who mourn for thee,
I alone must not weep. My office is
Henceforth to dry up tears, and not to shed them;
But yet of all who mourn, none mourn like me,
Not only for thyself, but him who slew thee.
Now, Cain! I will divide thy burden with thee.

CAIN - Eastward from Eden will we take our way;

'Tis the most desolate, and suits my steps.

ADAH - Lead! thou shalt be my guide, and may our God
Be thine! Now let us carry forth our children.

CAIN - And he who lieth there was childless! I
Have dried the fountain of a gentle race,
Which might have graced his recent marriage couch,
And might have tempered this stern blood of mine,
Uniting with our children Abel's offspring!
O Abel!

ADAH - Peace be with him!

CAIN - But with me!—

[Exeunt.

Lord Byron – A Short Biography

Byron, one of England's greatest poets, endured a quite difficult background. His father, Captain John "Mad Jack" Byron had married his second wife, the former Catherine Gordon, a descendant of Cardinal Beaton and heiress of the Gight estate in Aberdeenshire, Scotland for the same reason that he married his first: her money. Byron's mother-to-be had to sell her land and title to pay her new husband's debts and within two years the large estate of £23,500, had been squandered, leaving her with an annual income in trust of £150. In a move to avoid his creditors, Catherine accompanied her husband to France in 1786, but returned to England at the end of 1787 in order to give birth to her son on English soil.

George Gordon Byron was born on January 22nd 1788, in lodgings, at Holles Street in London although there is a conflicting account of him having been born in Dover.

He was christened, at St Marylebone Parish Church, George Gordon Byron, after his maternal grandfather, George Gordon of Gight, a descendant of James I of Scotland, who, in 1779, had committed suicide.

In 1790 Catherine moved back to Aberdeenshire and it was here that Byron spent his childhood. His father joined them in their lodgings in Queen Street, but the couple quickly separated. Catherine was prone to mood swings and melancholy. Her husband continued to borrow money from her and she fell deeper into debt. It was one of these "loans" that allowed him to travel to Valenciennes, France, where he died in 1791.

When Byron's great-uncle, the "wicked" Lord Byron, died on 21 May 1798, the 10-year-old boy became the 6th Baron Byron of Rochdale and inherited the ancestral home, Newstead Abbey, in Nottinghamshire. However the Abbey was in a state of disrepair and it was leased to Lord Grey de Ruthyn, and others for several years.

Catherine's parenting swung between either spoiling or indulging her son to stubbornly refusing every plea. Her drinking disgusted him, and he mocked her short and corpulent frame. She did retaliate and, in a fit of temper, once called him as "a lame brat", on account of his club-foot, an issue on which we was very sensitive. He referred to himself as "le diable boiteux" ("the limping devil").

Byron early education was taken at Aberdeen Grammar School, and in August 1799 he entered the school of Dr. William Glennie, in Dulwich. He was encouraged to exercise in moderation but could not restrain himself from "violent" bouts in an attempt to overcompensate for his deformed foot. His mother interfered, often withdrawing him from school, and resulting in him lacking discipline and neglecting his classical studies.

In 1801 he was sent to Harrow, where he remained until July 1805. Byron was an excellent orator but undistinguished student and an unskilled cricketer but strangely he did represent the school in the very first Eton v Harrow cricket match at Lord's in 1805.

Byron, always prone to over-indulge, fell in love with Mary Chaworth, whom he met while at school, and thence refused to return to Harrow in September 1803. His mother wrote, "He has no indisposition that I know of but love, desperate love, the worst of all maladies in my opinion. In short, the boy is distractedly in love with Miss Chaworth."

He did finally return in January 1804, and described his friends there; "My school friendships were with me passions for I was always violent." His nostalgic poems about his Harrow friendships, in his book Childish Recollections, published in 1806, talk of a "consciousness of sexual differences that may in the end make England untenable to him".

The following autumn he attended Trinity College, Cambridge, where he met and formed a close bond with John Edleston. On his "protégé" Byron wrote, "He has been my almost constant associate since October, 1805, when I entered Trinity College. His voice first attracted my attention, his countenance fixed it, and his manners attached me to him forever." In his memory Byron composed Thyrza, a series of elegies. In later years Byron described the affair as "a violent, though pure love and passion". The public were beginning to view homosexuality with increasing distaste and the law now specified such sanctions as public hanging against convicted or even suspected offenders. Though equally Byron may just be using 'pure' out of respect for Edleston's innocence, in contrast to the more sexually overt relations experienced at Harrow School. Byron is now thought of as bi-sexual though more fulfilled, on all levels, by women.

While not at school or college, Byron lived with his mother in Southwell, Nottinghamshire. While there, he cultivated friendships with Elizabeth Pigot and her brother, John, with whom he staged two plays for the entertainment of the local community. During this time, with the help of Elizabeth, who copied his rough drafts, he wrote his first volumes of poetry, Fugitive Pieces, which included poems written when Byron was only 14. However, it was promptly recalled and burned on the advice of his friend, the Reverend J. T. Becher, on account of its more amorous verses, particularly the poem To Mary.

Hours of Idleness, which collected many of the previous poems, along with recent compositions, was the culminating book. The savage, anonymous criticism this received in the Edinburgh Review prompted his first major satire, English Bards and Scotch Reviewers in 1809. This was put into the hands of his relative, R. C. Dallas, requesting him to "...get it published without his name". Although published anonymously Byron was generally known to be the author. The work so upset some of his critics they challenged Byron to a duel. Of course, over time, it became a mark of renown to be the target of Byron's pen.

Byron first took his seat in the House of Lords March 13th, 1809. He was a strong advocate of social reform, and one of the few Parliamentary defenders of the Luddites: specifically, he was against a death penalty for Luddite "frame breakers" in Nottinghamshire, who destroyed the textile machines that were putting them out of work. His first speech before the Lords, on February 27th, 1812, sarcastically referenced the "benefits" of automation, which he saw as producing inferior material as well as putting people out of work, and concluded the proposed law was only missing two things to be effective: "Twelve Butchers for a Jury and a Jeffries for a Judge!"

Two months later, Byron made another impassioned speech before the House in support of Catholic emancipation. He expressed opposition to the established religion because it was unfair to people who practiced other faiths.

Out of this period would follow several overtly political poems; Song for the Luddites (1816), The Landlords' Interest, Canto XIV of The Age of Bronze, Wellington: The Best of the Cut-Throats (1819) and The Intellectual Eunuch Castlereagh (1818).

Like his father Byron racked up numerous debts. His mother thought he had "reckless disregard for money" and lived in fear of her son's creditors.

Between1809 to 1811, Byron went on the Grand Tour, then customary for a young nobleman. The Napoleonic Wars meant most of Europe had to be avoided, and he instead ventured south to the Mediterranean.

There is some correspondence among his circle of Cambridge friends that suggests that another motive was the hope of homosexual experience, and other theories saying that he was worried about a possible dalliance with a married woman, Mary Chaworth, his former love.

But other possibilities exist. Byron had read much about the Ottoman and Persian lands as a child, was attracted to Islam (especially Sufi mysticism), and later wrote, "With these countries, and events connected with them, all my really poetical feelings begin and end."

Byron began his trip in Portugal from where he wrote a letter to his friend Mr. Hodgson in which he describes his mastery of the Portuguese language, consisting mainly of swearing and insults. Byron particularly enjoyed his stay in Sintra that is described in Childe Harold's Pilgrimage as "glorious Eden". From Lisbon he travelled overland to Seville, Jerez de la Frontera, Cádiz, Gibraltar and from there by sea on to Malta and Greece.

While in Athens, Byron met 14-year-old Nicolò Giraud, who became quite close and taught him Italian. Byron sent Giraud to school at a monastery in Malta and in his will, though later taken out, bequeathed him a sizeable sum.

Byron then moved on to Smyrna, and then Constantinople on board HMS Salsette. While HMS Salsette was anchored awaiting Ottoman permission to dock at the city, on May 3rd, 1810 Byron and Lieutenant Ekenhead, of Salsette 's Marines, swam the Hellespont. Byron commemorated this feat in the second canto of Don Juan.

When he sailed back to England in April 1811, he travelled, for a time, aboard the transport ship Hydra, which had on board the last large shipments of Lord Elgin's marbles, a piece of vandalism that Byron had longed railed against. The last leg of his voyage home was from Malta in aboard HMS Volage. He arrived at Sheerness, Kent, on July 14[th.] He was home after two years away.

On August 2nd, his mother died. "I had but one friend in the world," he exclaimed, "and she is gone."

The following year, 1812, Byron became a sensation with the publication, via his literary agent and family relative R. C. Dallas, of the first two cantos of 'Childe Harold's Pilgrimage'. He rapidly became the most brilliant star in the dazzling world of Regency London, sought after at every society venue, elected to several exclusive clubs, and frequented the most fashionable London drawing-rooms. His own words recall; "I awoke one morning and found myself famous". The Edinburgh Review allowed that Byron had "improved marvellously since his last appearance at our tribunal." He followed up his success with the poem's last two cantos, as well as four equally celebrated "Oriental Tales": The Giaour, The Bride of Abydos, The Corsair and Lara.

His affair with Lady Caroline Lamb (who called him "mad, bad and dangerous to know"), as well as other women and the constant pressure of debt, caused him to seek a suitable marriage i.e. marry wealth. One choice was Annabella Milbanke. But in 1813 he met again, after four years, his half-sister, Augusta Leigh. Rumours of incest constantly surrounded the pair; Augusta, who was married, gave birth on April 15th, 1814 to her third daughter, Elizabeth Medora Leigh, and Byron is suspected to be the father.

To escape from debts and rumours he now sought, in earnest, to marry Annabella, (said to be the likely heiress of a rich uncle). They married on January 2nd, 1815, and their daughter, Ada, was born in December of that year. However Byron's continuing obsession with Augusta and dalliances with others made their marriage a misery.

Annabella thought Byron insane and she left him, taking Ada, in January 1816 and began proceedings for a legal separation. For Byron the scandal of the separation, the continuing rumours about Augusta, and ever-increasing debts were to now force him to leave England.

He passed through Belgium and along the river Rhine and by the summer was settled at the Villa Diodati by Lake Geneva, Switzerland, with his personal physician, the young, brilliant, and handsome John William Polidori. There Byron befriended the poet Percy Bysshe Shelley, and his future wife Mary Godwin. He was also joined by Mary's stepsister, Claire Clairmont, with whom, almost inevitably, he had had an affair with in London.

Kept indoors at the Villa Diodati by the incessant rain during three days in June, the five turned to writing. Mary Shelley produced what would become Frankenstein, or The Modern Prometheus, and Polidori was inspired by a fragmentary story of Byron's, Fragment of a Novel, to produce The Vampyre, the progenitor of the romantic vampire genre.

Byron's story fragment was published as a postscript to Mazeppa; he also now wrote the third canto of Childe Harold.

Byron wintered in Venice, pausing his travels when he fell in love with Marianna Segati, in whose Venice house he was lodging, but who was soon replaced by 22-year-old Margarita Cogni; both women were married. Cogni, who could not read or write, left her husband to move into Byron's Venice house. Their fighting often caused Byron to spend nights in his gondola; when he asked her to leave the house, she threw herself into the Venetian canal.

In a visit to San Lazzaro degli Armeni in Venice, he began to immerse himself in Armenian culture. He learned the Armenian language, and attended many seminars about language and history. He co-authored English Grammar and Armenian in 1817, and Armenian Grammar and English in 1819, where he included quotations from classical and modern Armenian and later, in 1821, participated in the compilation of the English Armenian dictionary, and in the preface he mapped out the relationship of the Armenians with, and the oppression of, the Turkish "pashas" and the Persian satraps, and their struggle for liberation.

In 1817 after a visit to Rome and back in Venice, he wrote the fourth canto of Childe Harold and sold his ancestral home, Newstead Abbey, as well as publishing Manfred; A Dramatic Poem and , Cain; A Mystery.

Byron wrote the first five cantos of his renowned Don Juan between 1818 and 1820. And besides work and adventure there was always love. Women, of course, were always in evidence and the young Countess Teresa Guiccioli found her first love in Byron, who in turn asked her to elope with him. They lived in Ravenna between 1819 and 1821 where he continued Don Juan and also wrote the Ravenna Diary, My Dictionary and Recollections.

It was here that he now received visits from Percy Bysshe Shelley and Thomas Moore.

Of Byron's lifestyle in Ravenna Shelley informs us that; "Lord Byron gets up at two. I get up, quite contrary to my usual custom ... at 12. After breakfast we sit talking till six. From six to eight we gallop through the pine forest which divide Ravenna from the sea; we then come home and dine, and sit up gossiping till six in the morning. I don't suppose this will kill me in a week or fortnight, but I shall not try it longer. Lord B.'s establishment consists, besides servants, of ten horses, eight enormous dogs, three monkeys, five cats, an eagle, a crow, and a falcon; and all these, except the horses, walk about the house, which every now and then resounds with their unarbitrated quarrels, as if they were the masters of it... . [P.S.] I find that my enumeration of the animals in this Circean Palace was defective .... I have just met on the grand staircase five peacocks, two guinea hens, and an Egyptian crane. I wonder who all these animals were before they were changed into these shapes."

From 1821 to 1822, he finished Cantos 6–12 of Don Juan at Pisa, and in the same year he joined with Leigh Hunt and Percy Bysshe Shelley in starting a short-lived newspaper, The Liberal, in the first number of which appeared The Vision of Judgment.

For the first time since his arrival in Italy, Byron found himself tempted to give dinner parties; his guests included the Shelleys, Edward Ellerker Williams, Thomas Medwin, John Taaffe and Edward John Trelawney; and "never", as Shelley said, "did he display himself to more advantage than on these occasions; being at once polite and cordial, full of social hilarity and the most perfect good humour; never diverging into ungraceful merriment, and yet keeping up the spirit of liveliness throughout the evening."

Byron's mother-in-law Judith Noel, the Hon. Lady Milbanke, died in 1822. Her will required that he change his surname to "Noel" in order for him to inherit half of her estate. He obtained a Royal Warrant allowing him to "take and use the surname of Noel only". The Royal Warrant also allowed him to "subscribe the said surname of Noel before all titles of honour", and from that point he signed himself "Noel Byron" (the usual signature of a peer being merely the peerage, in this case simply "Byron").

The Shelley's and Williams had rented a house on the coast and had a schooner built. Byron decided that he too should have his own yacht, and engaged Trelawny's friend, Captain Daniel Roberts, to design and construct the boat. It was named the Bolivar.

On July 8th, 1822 Shelley drowned in a boating accident. Byron attended the funeral. Shelley was cremated on the beach at Viareggio where his body had washed up. His ashes were later interred in Rome in the cemetery in Rome where lay already his son William and John Keats.

Byron was living in Genoa when, in 1823, while growing bored, he accepted a call for his help from representatives of the movement for Greek independence from the Ottoman Empire. With the assistance of his banker and Captain Daniel Roberts, Byron chartered the Brig Hercules to take him to Greece. On 16 July, Byron left Genoa arriving at Kefalonia in the Ionian Islands on August 4th.

Byron had spent £4,000 of his own money to refit the Greek fleet and sailed for Missolonghi in western Greece, arriving on December 29th, to join Alexandros Mavrokordatos, a Greek politician with military power. When the famous Danish sculptor Bertel Thorvaldsen heard about Byron's heroics in Greece, he voluntarily re-sculpted his earlier bust of Byron in Greek marble.

Mavrokordatos and Byron planned to attack the Turkish-held fortress of Lepanto, at the mouth of the Gulf of Corinth. Byron employed a fire-master to prepare artillery and took part of the rebel army under his own command, despite his lack of military experience. Before the expedition could sail, on February 15th, 1824, he fell ill, and the usual remedy of bloodletting weakened him further. He made a partial recovery, but in early April he caught a violent cold which further therapeutic bleeding, insisted on by his doctors, aggravated. He developed a violent fever, and died in Missolonghi on April 19th.

Alfred, Lord Tennyson would later recall the shocked reaction in Britain when word was received of Byron's death. The Greeks mourned Lord Byron deeply, and he became a hero. The Greek form of "Byron", continues in popularity as a name in Greece, and a town near Athens is called Vyronas in his honour.

Byron's body was embalmed, but the Greeks wanted their hero to stay with them. Some say his heart was removed to remain in Missolonghi. His body was returned to England (despite his dying wishes that it should not) for burial in Westminster Abbey, but the Abbey refused to accept it on the grounds of "questionable morality".

Huge crowds viewed his body as he lay in state for two days in London before being buried at the Church of St. Mary Magdalene in Hucknall, Nottinghamshire. A marble slab given by the King of Greece is laid directly above Byron's grave.

Byron's friends had raised the sum of £1,000 to commission a statue of the writer by the sculptor Thorvaldsen. However for a decade after the statue was completed, in 1834, most British institutions had refused to accept it, among them the British Museum, St. Paul's Cathedral, Westminster Abbey and the National Gallery, and it remained in storage. Finally Trinity College, Cambridge, placed the statue in its library.

Finally, in 1969, a145 years after Byron's death, a memorial to him was placed in Westminster Abbey. It had been pointedly noted by the New York Times that "People are beginning to ask whether this ignoring of Byron is not a thing of which England should be ashamed ... a bust or a tablet might be put in the Poets' Corner and England be relieved of ingratitude toward one of her really great sons." At last Byron was where he should be.

Answer to the Foregoing, Addressed to Miss —
Aristomenes
Away, Away, Ye Notes of Woe!

B
Ballad
Beppo, a Venetian Story
The Blues, a Literary Eclogue
Bowles and Campbell
The Bride of Abydos, a Turkish Tale (A transcription project)
Bright Be the Place of Thy Soul! (see "Stanzas for Music")
By the Rivers of Babylon We Sat Down and Wept
"By the Waters of Babylon"

C
Cain, a Mystery (A transcription project)
The Chain I gave (same as "From the Turkish")
The Charity Ball
Childe Harold's Good Night (from Childe Harold's Pilgrimage, Canto I.)
Childe Harold's Pilgrimage
Childish Recollections
Churchill's Grave
The Conquest
The Cornelian
The Corsair: A Tale
The Curse of Minerva

D
Damætas
Darkness
The Death of Calmar and Orla
The Deformed Transformed, a drama (A transcription project)
The Destruction of Sennacherib
The Devil's Drive
Don Juan
A Dream (same as "Darkness")
The Dream
The Duel

E
E Nihilo Nihil; or, An Epigram Bewitched
Egotism. A Letter to J. T. Becher
Elegiac Stanzas on the Death of Sir Peter Parker, Bart.
Elegy
Elegy on Newstead Abbey
Elegy on the Death of Sir Peter Parker (same "Elegiac Stanzas on the Death of Sir Peter Parker, Bart.")
Endorsement to the Deed of Separation, in the April of 1816
English Bards, and Scotch Reviewers, a Satire
Epigram (If for Silver, or for Gold)
Epigram (In Digging up your Bones, Tom Paine)
Epigram (It Seems That the Braziers Propose Soon to Pass)

Epigram (The world is a bundle of hay)
Epigram on an Old Lady Who Had Some Curious Notions Respecting the Soul
Epigrams (Oh, Castlereagh! Thou Art a Patriot Now)
Epilogue
The Episode of Nisus and Euryalus (A Paraphrase from the Æneid, Lib. 9.)
Epistle from Mr. Murray to Dr. Polidori
Epistle to a Friend
Epistle to Augusta
Epistle to Mr. Murray
Epitaph
Epitaph for Joseph Blacket, Late Poet and Shoemaker
Epitaph for William Pitt
Epitaph on a Beloved Friend
Epitaph on a Friend (same as "Epitaph on a Beloved Friend")
Epitaph on John Adams, of Southwell
Epitaph to a Dog
Euthanasia

F

Fame, Wisdom, Love, and Power Were Mine (same as "All is Vanity, saith the Preacher")
Fare Thee Well
Farewell (same as "Farewell! if Ever Fondest Prayer")
Farewell Petition to J. C. H., Esqre.
Farewell to Malta
Farewell to the Muse
Fill the Goblet Again
The First Kiss of Love
A Fragment (Could I Remount the River of My Years)
Fragment (Hills of Annesley, Bleak and Barren)
A Fragment (When, to Their Airy Hall, my Fathers' Voice)
Fragment from the "Monk of Athos"
Fragment of a Translation from the 9th Book of Virgil's Æneid (compare "The Episode of Nisus and Euryalus")
Fragment of an Epistle to Thomas Moore
Fragments of School Exercises: From the "Prometheus Vinctus" of Æschylus
Francesca of Rimini
Francisca
From Anacreon Ode 3. ('Twas Now the Hour When Night Had Driven)
From Job (same as "A Spirit Passed Before Me")
From the French (Ægle, Beauty and Poet, Has Two Little Crimes)
From the French (Must Thou Go, my Glorious Chief)
From the Last Hill That Looks on Thy Once Holy Dome (same as "On the Day of the Destruction of Jerusalem by Titus")
From the Portuguese
From the Turkish (same as "The Chain I Gave")

G

G. G. B. to E. P. (same as "To M. S. G.") (When I Dream That You Love Me, you'll surely Forgive)
The Giaour
The Girl of Cadiz
Granta. A Medley

Lines Written Beneath an Elm in the Churchyard of Harrow
Lines Written in an Album, At Malta
Lines Written in "Letters of an Italian Nun and an English Gentleman
Lines Written on a Blank Leaf of The Pleasures of Memory
Lord Byron's Verses on Sam Rogers
Love and Death
Love and Gold
A Love Song. To — (same as "Remind me not, Remind me not")
Love's Last Adieu
Lucietta. A Fragment

M

Maid of Athens, Ere We Part
Manfred, a Dramatic Poem
Marino Faliero, Doge of Venice, an Historical Tragedy (1821) (A transcription project)
Martial, Lib. I. Epig. I.
Mazeppa
Monody on the Death of the Right Hon. R. B. Sheridan
The Morgante Maggiore (A transcription project)
My Boy Hobbie O
My Epitaph
My Soul is Dark

N

Napoleon's Farewell
Napoleon's Snuff-box
The New Vicar of Bray
Newstead Abbey

O

An Occasional Prologue
Ode from the French
Ode on Venice
Ode to a Lady Whose Lover was Killed by a Ball, Which at the Same Time Shivered a Portrait Next His Heart
Ode to Napoleon Buonaparte
An Ode to the Framers of the Frame Bill
Oh! Snatched Away in Beauty's Bloom
Oh! Weep for Those
On a Change of Masters at a Great Public School
On a Cornelian Heart Which Was Broken
On a Distant View of the Village and School of Harrow on the Hill, 1806
On a Royal Visit to the Vaults (Windsor Poetics)
On Being Asked What Was the "Origin of Love"
On Finding a Fan
On Jordan's Banks
On Leaving Newstead Abbey
On Lord Thurlow's Poems
On Moore's Last Operatic Farce, or Farcical Opera
On My Thirty-third Birthday
On My Wedding-Day

On Napoleon's Escape from Elba
On Parting
On Revisiting Harrow
On Sam Rogers (same as "Lord Byron's Verses on Sam Rogers")
On the Birth of John William Rizzo Hoppner
On the Bust of Helen by Canova
On the Day of the Destruction of Jerusalem by Titus
On the Death of — Thyrza (same as "To Thyrza")
On the Death of a Young Lady
On the Death of Mr. Fox
On the Death of the Duke of Dorset
On the Eyes of Miss A— H—
On the Quotation
On the Star of "the Legion of Honour"
On this Day I complete my Thirty-sixth Year
One Struggle More, and I Am Free
Oscar of Alva
Ossian's Address to the Sun in "Carthon"

P

Parenthetical Address
Parisina
Pignus Amoris
The Prayer of Nature
The Prisoner of Chillon
The Prophecy of Dante, a Poem

Q

Quem Deus Vult Perdere Prius Dementat
Queries to Casuists

R

R. C. Dallas
Remember Him, whom Passion's Power
Remember Thee! Remember thee!
Remembrance
Remind Me Not, Remind Me Not
Reply to Some Verses of J. M. B. Pigot, Esq., on the Cruelty of his Mistress

S

Sardanapalus, a Tragedy (A transcription project)
Saul
She Walks in Beauty
The Siege of Corinth
A Sketch From Life
So We'll Go No More A-Roving
Soliloquy of a Bard in the Country
Sonetto di Vittorelli
Song (Breeze of the Night in Gentler Sighs)
Song (Fill the Goblet Again! For I Never Before)
Song (Maid of Athens, Ere We Part) (same as "Maid of Athens, Ere We Part")

Song (Thou Art Not False, But Thou Art fickle) same as "Thou Art Not False, But Thou Art Fickle")
Song (When I Roved a Young Highlander) (same as "When I Roved a Young Highlander")
Song For the Luddites
Song of Saul Before His Last Battle
Song To the Suliotes
Sonnet On Chillon
Sonnet on the Nuptials of the Marquis Antonio Cavalli with the Countess Clelia Rasponi of Ravenna
Sonnet, to Genevra (Thine eyes' Blue Tenderness, Thy Long Fair Hair)
Sonnet, to Generva (Thy Cheek is Pale with Thought, but Not From Woe). aka "Sonnet, to the Same"
Sonnet to Lake Leman
Sonnet to the Prince Regent
The Spell is Broke, the Charm is Flown!
A Spirit Passed Before Me
Stanzas (And Thou Art Dead, as Young and Fair)
Stanzas (And Wilt Thou Weep When I am Low?) (same as "And Wilt Thou Weep When I Am Low?")
Stanzas (Away, Away, Ye Notes of Woe)
Stanzas (Chill and Mirk is the Nightly Blast) (same as "Stanzas Composed During a Thunderstorm")
Stanzas (Could Love For Ever)
Stanzas (I Would I Were a Careless Child) (same as "I Would I Were a Careless Child")
Stanzas (If Sometimes in the Haunts of Men)
Stanzas (One Struggle More, and I Am Free)
Stanzas (Remember Him, Whom Passion's Power)
Stanzas (Thou Art Not False, but Thou Art Fickle)
Stanzas (Through Cloudless Skies, in Silvery Sheen) (same as "Stanzas Written in Passing the Ambracian Gulf")
Stanzas (When a Man Hath No Freedom to Fight For at Home)
Stanzas Composed During a Thunderstorm
Stanzas For Music (Bright Be the Place of Thy Soul!)
Stanzas For Music (I Speak Not, I Trace Not, I Breathe Not Thy Name)
Stanzas For Music (There Be None of Beauty's Daughters)
Stanzas For Music (There's Not a Joy the World Can Give Like That it Takes Away)
Stanzas For Music (They Say That Hope is Happiness)
Stanzas To — (same as "Stanzas to Augusta": Though the Day of My Destiny's Over)
Stanzas To a Hindoo Air
Stanzas To a Lady, on Leaving England
Stanzas To a Lady, with the Poems of Camoëns
Stanzas To Augusta (When all around grew drear and dark)
Stanzas To Augusta (Though the day of my Destiny's over)
Stanzas To Jessy
Stanzas To the Po
Stanzas To the Same (same as "There was a Time, I need not name")
Stanzas Written in Passing the Ambracian Gulf
Stanzas Written on the Road Between Florence and Pisa
Substitute For an Epitaph
Sun of the Sleepless!
Sympathetic Address to a Young Lady (same as "Lines to a Lady Weeping")

T
The Tear
There Be None of Beauty's Daughters (see "Stanzas for Music")
There Was a Time, I Need Not Name

There's Not a Joy the World Can Give Like That it Takes Away (see "Stanzas for Music")
They say that Hope is Happiness (see "Stanzas for Music")
Thou Art Not False, but Thou Art Fickle
Thou Whose Spell Can Raise the Dead (same as "Saul")
Thoughts Suggested by a College Examination
Thy Days are Done
To — (But Once I Dared to Lift My Eyes)
To — (Oh! Well I Know Your Subtle Sex)
To A— (same as "To M—")
To a Beautiful Quaker
To a Knot of Ungenerous Critics
To a Lady (Oh! Had My Fate Been Join'd with Thine)
To a Lady (This Band, Which Bound Thy yellow Hair)
To a Lady (When Man, Expell'd from Eden's Bowers)
To a Lady Weeping (same as "Lines To a Lady Weeping")
To a Lady who Presented to the Author a Lock of Hair Braided with His Own, and Appointed a Night
in December to Meet Him in the Garden
To a Vain Lady
To a Youthful Friend
To an Oak at Newstead
To Anne (Oh, Anne, Your Offences to Me Have Been Grievous)
To Anne (Oh Say Not, Sweet Anne, That the Fates Have Decreed)
To Belshazzar
To Caroline (Oh! When Shall the Grave Hide For Ever My Sorrow?)
To Caroline (Think'st thou I saw thy beauteous eyes)
To Caroline (When I Hear you Express an Affection so Warm)
To Caroline (You Say You Love, and Yet Your Eye)
To D—
To Dives. A Fragment
To E—
To Edward Noel Long, Esq.
To Eliza
To Emma
To E. N. L. Esq. (same as "To Edward Noel Long, Esq.")
To Florence
To George Anson Byron (?)
To George, Earl Delawarr
To Harriet
To Ianthe (The "Origin of Love!"—Ah, why) (same as "On Being Asked What Was the 'Origin of
Love'")
To Ianthe (from Canto I of Childe Harold's Pilgrimage) (Not in Those Climes Where I Have Late Been
Straying)
To Inez (from Canto I of Childe Harold's Pilgrimage) (Nay, Smile Not at My Sullen Brow)
To Julia (same as "To Lesbia!")
To Lesbia!
To Lord Thurlow
To M—
To Maria — (same as "To Emma")
To Mrs. — (same as "Well! Thou Art Happy")
To Mrs. Musters (same as "Stanzas To a Lady, On Leaving England")
To M. S. G. (When I Dream That You Love Me, You'll Surely Forgive)

To M. S. G. (Whene'er I View Those Lips of Thine)
To Marion
To Mary, on Receiving Her Picture
To Miss E. P. (same as "To Eliza")
To Mr. Murray (For Orford and for Waldegrave)
To Mr. Murray (Strahan, Tonson, Lintot of the Times)
To Mr. Murray (To Hook the Reader, You, John Murray)
To my Son
To Penelope
To Romance
To Samuel Rogers, Esq. (same as "Lines Written On a Blank Leaf of The Pleasures of Memory")
To Sir W. D. (same as "To a Youthful Friend")
To the Author of a Sonnet
To the Countess of Blessington
To the Duke of D— (same as "To the Duke of Dorset")
To the Duke of Dorset
To the Earl of — (same as "To the Earl of Clare")
To the Earl of Clare
To the Honble. Mrs. George Lamb
To the Prince Regent on the Repeal of the Bill of Attainder Against Lord E. Fitzgerald, June, 1819. (same as "Sonnet to the Prince Regent")
To the Rev. J. T. Becher (same as "Lines: Addressed to the Rev. J. T. Becher")
To the Same (same as "And Wilt Thou Weep When I Am Low?")
To the Sighing Strephon
To Thomas Moore (My Boat is on the Shore)
To Thomas Moore (Oh you, Who in all Names Can Tickle the Town)
To Thomas Moore (What Are You Doing Now)
To Thyrza (Without a Stone to Mark the Spot)
To Thyrza (One Struggle More, and I Am Free) (same as "One Struggle More, and I am Free")
To Time
To Woman
Translation from Anacreon Ode 1. (I Wish to Tune My Quivering Lyre)
Translation from Anacreon Ode 5. (Mingle with the Genial Bowl)
Translation from Catullus: Ad Lesbiam
Translation from Catullus: Lugete Veneres Cupidinesque
Translation from Horace
Translation from the "Medea" of Euripides [Ll. 627–660]
Translation from Vittorelli
Translation of a Romaic Love Song
Translation of the Epitaph on Virgil and Tibullus, by Domitius Marsus
Translation of the Famous Greek War Song
Translation of the Nurse's Dole in the Medea of Euripides
Translation of the Romaic Song
The Two Foscari, a Tragedy (A transcription project)

U

V
Venice. A Fragment
Verses Found in a Summer-house at Hales-Owen
Versicles

A Version of Ossian's Address to the Sun
A very Mournful Ballad on the Siege and Conquest of Alhama
Vision of Belshazzar
The Vision of Judgment (A transcription project)
A Volume of Nonsense

W

The Waltz, an Apostrophic Hymn
Warriors and Chiefs! (same as "Song of Saul Before His Last Battle")
We Sate Down and Wept by the Waters of Babel (same as "By the Rivers of Babylon We Sat Down and Wept")
Well! Thou art Happy
Were My Bosom as False as Thou Deem'st It To Be
Werner, or The Inheritance, a Tragedy (A transcription project)
When a Man Hath No Freedom to Fight For at Home (see "Stanzas")
When Coldness Wraps This Suffering Clay
When I Roved a Young Highlander
When We Two Parted
The Wild Gazelle
Windsor Poetics
A Woman's Hair
Written after Swimming from Sestos to Abydos
Written at Athens (same as "The Spell is Broke, the Charm is Flown!")
Written at the Request of a Lady in her Memorandum Book (same as "Lines Written in an Album, At Malta")
Written in an Album (same as "Lines Written in an Album, At Malta")
Written in Mrs. Spencer S.'s— (same as "Lines Written in an Album, At Malta")

Made in the USA
Middletown, DE
17 May 2022

65898317R00046